Scotlands, 2 1994

© Edinburgh University Press 1995

Typeset in Berkeley Old Style by
Bibliocraft, Dundee
and printed and bound in Great Britain
by Page Bros Ltd, Norwich, Norfolk

A CIP record is available

ISSN 1350–7508

Scotlands is supported by the St Andrews Scottish Studies Institute,
University of St Andrews, and the Scottish Studies Association, University
of Waikato, New Zealand

DOUGLAS DUNN

The Representation of Women in Scottish literature

When I began to think about what I might find to say on this subject I first of all allowed myself to wander in a mental anthology of poems and fiction in which women are prominent. What came to mind were such works as Henryson's *Testament of Cresseid*, *Aeneid* IV in Gavin Douglas's translation, and William Dunbar's 'The Tretis of the Tua Mariit Wemen and the Wedo'. The Ballads recommended themselves as important. So, too, did carnivalesque poems such as 'Peblis to the Play' and their eighteenth-century derivatives by Ramsay, Fergusson and Burns, in the gaiety of which social inclusiveness is brusque but also significant. Burns's love poetry and songs looked like an obvious district to be explored, as did Scott's novels. J. M. Barrie's *Margaret Ogilvy*, or a play like *The Twelve Pound Look*, and Grassic Gibbon's story 'Smeddum' as well as *A Scots Quair*, pressed themselves forward for attention. Twentieth-century writing by women preoccupied me for some time, too – Catherine Carswell, Willa Muir, Naomi Mitchison, Muriel Spark, Elspeth Davie, as well as neglected figures like Violet Jacob, the two Findlater sisters, Lorna Moon, Rachel Annand Taylor and Dorothy K. Haynes; and I felt anxious to say something about the more numerous younger writers, such as Janice Galloway, A. L. Kennedy, Dilys Rose and Liz Lochhead, among others. But what began to emerge more clearly from my reading was the extent to which Scottish literature was, and is, controlled by male psychologies, and the extent to which characters like Gibbon's Meg Menzies (in 'Smeddum') and Chris Guthrie seek sub-conscious compensation – on the author's behalf – for the social and cultural pressures which determine their lives and circum-stances. In writing by men, a positive female character can operate in a manner that comes close to cultural apology.

Feminist criticism, it seems to me, is not just 'best left to women'. On the part of a critic who is a man, that abdication of critical rights is obligatory – but only if the male critic takes care to maintain *his* sensible involvement in what is *hers*. Let me put it this way in an attempt to be absolutely clear about what I mean. Any man who has a mother, a wife, a sister, or a daughter, ought to raise his voice, not to 'protect' them from cultural hurt – nothing as patriarchal and condescending as that – but to remove the possible sources of cultural harm from society. Essentially, it's a question of getting things right in your own head. For a male Scottish writer and critic this is extremely important business. In Scottish literature, I feel – because I can't prove it – that the true responsibility is to save it from itself, from damaging cultural, social and political pressures. Prominent among these is a range of characteristic attitudes to women. For we take part in the literature that gave the world 'Tam O Shanter', *Treasure Island*, *The Strange Case of Dr Jekyll and Mr Hyde*, *A Drunk Man Looks at the Thistle*, 'On a Raised Beach', and *Peter Pan*. In one way or another these are all adventure stories for boys. They are not 'about' the masculine psyche; they are its disclosures. They are works of flight, but not 'from the enchantress fleeing'; or perhaps that *is* what they are – farewells to a world both domestic and universal in which women play a central role, except that in these works women don't. They are masterpieces; they are also monuments either of the relatively womanless (Stevenson's two stories), or of male-centred psycho-sexual turbulence (parts of *A Drunk Man*), or of mania determined by alcohol, or, in the case of 'On a Raised Beach', of geo-metaphysical rhapsodics engaged in for the sake of a narcissistic betterment and strengthening of the will and its powers of resolve. Other than the poet, there are no *people* in that poem. *Peter Pan* just defeats me. Its story sings in my blood, but I know that if I manage to paraphrase it coherently then on that day I'll be able to fly. Quite simply, it speaks of the boyhood that survives in every man, and that is no more to be relinquished than the girlhood that survives in every woman. The truth of *Peter Pan* is bio-neurological. To deny it is to reveal oneself as a prig.

A subject such as this one is hazardous in that it can risk distorting individual works through bringing to bear the weight of what are topical and personal urgencies now, but which weren't then. Revising the canon of literature is one thing. The revision of literature itself – what it is permitted to say, how it is said, the actual writing of it, here and now – is something else entirely. That is the proper business of poets, novelists, short-story writers, and playwrights, not of critics and theorists, except where the creative and critical overlap. Even then, advocacy usually opens itself to grounds for suspicion. Post-dated advocacy is just as bad, though, whether from critic or theorist, or the poet- or novelist-critic, or anyone else. Literature exists in its own time, as well as ours. As readers, we learn how to suspend disbelief, or not, as the case may be. Neither of these mental or imaginative activities need involve intellectual or moral torture or indignation. Not only is it silly to try to kick a long-dead author, it's impossible, while sticking pins in effigies is equally banal.

There seems very little point in complaining about the scarcity of women in Barbour's *The Bruce*. But it is the only poem in Scottish literature with a claim to being the national epic. How women are represented in it, is, therefore, of some interest, even if *The Bruce* is now remote from readers and remembered only for a few stirring lines on freedom. Conditioned by the temporal priorities of the late fourteenth century, at least as these prevailed in Scotland, it is a form of *chanson de geste*. Over its almost 14,000 lines it is more taken up with military events, the redemption of the kingdom, the establishment of a dynasty, and such concepts as freedom, valour, loyalty, self-sacrifice, and fate, than the right rendering of the sexes.

For example, King Robert I's Queen is mentioned twice, first when she is captured along with her daughter Marjory, and given to the English, and later when they are released through an exchange of prisoners after Bannockburn. Barbour says nothing of their captivity other than that Bishop Robert (of Glasgow) has been blinded during it. Others had been cruelly executed. However, Bruce's sister was ill-treated in a major way, as we are told in Professor Barrow's account – she was kept in a cage in Roxburgh castle. The Queen was confined in the manor house at Burstwick in the East Riding of Yorkshire. Her more comfortable captivity is explained by her reluctance to be a queen at all – but Barbour passes over this unpatriotic royal truculence. These seem strange omissions, but they are explained by the tendency of the *chanson de geste* to pass over embarrassing details, or the horrors of war, with the exception of transgressions on the military code inflicted on noble male participants. In Book VII there is an episode in which an English commander sends a female spy into the Bruce's camp shortly before the battle at Loch Trool in Galloway. Either this is historical, or legendary, or an anecdotal device to bring out the Bruce's acumen – he no sooner sees the woman than his suspicions are aroused. In Book XVI, when King Robert is campaigning in Ireland, a laundress in his camp is discovered to be about to give birth to a child. Again, this looks like an opportunity for spotlighting kingly courtesy and concern. He puts up a tent for her and delays his next march until the woman is safely through labour, the implication being that King Robert lost Ireland as the result of an act of humanity. Elsewhere, Bruce enters incognito into the house of a peasant woman. The incident then sets out to show his common touch and the love felt for him by the people. Lacking a single soldier with him, the woman enlists her two sons forthwith. A moment later, they're joined by Sir Edward Bruce, the Black Douglas and a hundred and fifty others. And that is virtually the entire female cast in what is a very long poem.

Barbour was born around 1320, and *The Bruce* written probably around 1375. When we bear in mind that the poetry of the Troubadours flourished between 1100 and the mid-fourteenth century, that Dante died in 1321, that Petrarch was born in 1303, Boccaccio born about 1313, and Chaucer in 1340, then, without devaluing the Scottish poet's work, we might begin to sense something of its relatively unsophisticated mode, or the extent to which it relies on an expressive ideal already overtaken elsewhere in Europe. Part of that change in European poetry was generated by an idealizing, but also active, erotic contemplation of women – indeed, it has been described as 'the invention of love' itself, in the twelfth century. Two of the great love stories of European poetry are of around this time – that of Dante and Beatrice, and Petrarch and Laura. We tend to think of Scottish poetry as devoid of such near-legendary poetic loves; but *The Kingis Quair*, probably written between the mid to late 1420s, can be seen as such a love story, that of James I and Joan Beaufort. Assuming James I to have been the author of the poem, he had the benefit of Chaucer's influence, as well as Lydgate's. That is, James I enjoyed access to erotic ideas which were either not the concern of Barbour, or of which he was ignorant, or contemptuous.

Women were important subjects to mediaeval writers – Boccaccio's *Concerning Famous Women*, for example, as well as his *Decameron*, Chaucer's *The Book of the Duchess* (1369), *Troilus and Criseyde* (1382–5), *The Legend of Good Women* (1385–6), and some famous stories in *The Canterbury Tales*. In France, Christine de Pizan wrote two important works, *The City of Ladies* (1404) and *The Treasure of the City of Ladies* (1405), sometimes called *Book of the Three Virtues*. Broad in their social range, and sometimes realistic, sometimes conventional, Christine de Pizan's writings reveal her critical attitude towards the position of women in French society. She can even be thought of as a proto-feminist literary critic in that she disagreed with prevailing opinion on how women were represented in the *Roman de la Rose*.

Christine de Pizan is virtually unique. Certainly, she has no identifiable Scottish counterpart. In her acknowledgement as one of the first women to earn her livelihood from authorship, we get some sense of her exceptional prestige as well as the unpropitious circumstances for other perhaps equally gifted women of her time. From the point of view of Scotland and its court culture, it seems reasonable to take it for granted that these circumstances were much the same as elsewhere but probably worse. To go much further than that is to fall into the old pessimistic error of defining Scottish literature by what it doesn't have – it doesn't have a Shakespeare or the equivalent of Elizabethan and Jacobean poetic drama. It doesn't have a Milton. It doesn't have a Wordsworth, or a Dickens, or a George Eliot, or a Jane Austen, or an Elizabeth Barrett Browning. Literatures are best defined by what they have and not by their lacunae, which, in any case, are almost always explicable in one way or another. But if, as I suspect, and as I now speculate, the poetic invention of love by the Troubadours was late in arriving in Scotland, then that belated encounter with Romantic love could be significant.

Henryson's version of the Cresseid story differs from Chaucer's, not only in scale, but in the intensity with which the Scottish poet concentrates his focus. His poem evokes a woman's vulnerability before the mischief of her own decisions, and those of men, (including authors), Cupid, Venus (the ciphers of love and sexuality), and the inter-planetary mayhem of Fortuna astrologically expressed. In a dream, Cresseid witnesses the judgement and punishment lavished on her by supernatural powers. Saturn speaks:

> 'I change thy mirth into melancholy
> Quhilk is the mother of all pensiveness;
> Thy moisture and thy heit in cald and dry;
> Thyne insolence, thy play and wantones
> To greit diseis; thy pomp and thy riches
> In mortall neid; and greit penuritie
> Thow suffer sall, and as ane beggar die.'

We might worry about the poetic psychology – whether individual or collective or conventional – which makes it possible for a venomous curse to be delivered with such force. But whatever vindictive relish is to be found in Saturn's lines is complicated by the poet-narrator's intervention in the next stanza:

> O cruell Saturne, fraward and angrie,
> Hard is thy dome and to malitious!
> On fair Cresseid quhy hes thow na mercie,
> Quhilk was sa sweit, gentill and amorous?
> Withdraw thy sentence and be gracious –
> As thow was never; sa schawis thow thy deid
> Ane wraikfull sentence gevin on fair Cresseid.

Punish her, he says, but not so severely as all that. Much of the time it is possible to feel that Henryson regrets being boxed in by the established boundaries of his story. Misfortune, and horror, are interpolated by the poet's dismay, with the result that he appears impatient with the inevitabilities of the drama he is retelling, like someone translating a poem they neither like nor agree with. At least part of the poem's passionate dynamic, although it is submerged, and scarcely conscious of itself, is

Henryson's unwillingness to accept that Cresseid's punishment is deserved. Reading *The Testament* you can feel yourself believe that Henryson would rather see the story in terms more clearly of what men do to women and women do to men. The conveniently expressive terms of how divine agents step in with dreadful punishments for those who transgress on the erotic regulations are his expressive means, and he uses them with pathos and panache. But you can find yourself wondering if Henryson is content with them, and if he is longing for, or dreaming of, a realism which could dispense with conventional properties. Despite that, however, Henryson's description of Cresseid's mutilation carries with it a conviction in the rightness of the punishment as well as distrust of its extremity:

> 'Fra heit of bodie I the now depryve,
> And to thy seiknes sall be na recure,
> Bot in dolour thy dayis to indure.
>
> 'Thy cristall ene minglit with blude I mak;
> Thy voice sa cleir, unplesand, hoir and hace;
> Thy lustie lyre ouirspred with spottis blak,
> And lumpis haw appeirand in thy face;
> Quhair thow cummis ilk man sall fle the place;
> This sall thow go begging fra hous to hous
> With cop and clapper lyke ane lazarous.'

Although the emotional dynamic of the poem verges on an ambiguity of purpose, an uncertainty of focus, the closing lines of *The Complaint of Cresseid* place it firmly within the hortatory ethics of its time.

> Now, worthie wemen, in this ballet schort,
> Maid for your worschip and instructioun,
> Of cherite, I monische and exhort:
> Ming not your lufe with fals deceptioun.
> Beir in your mynd this schort conclusioun
> Of fair Cresseid – as I have said befoir;
> Sen scho is deid, I speik of her no moir.

That last line is surely an appeal to the reticence and forgiveness of the common heart. As such, it is a cancellation of the horror that has gone before.

No one would call Henryson a feminist, or even tending in that direction; but his moral spokesmanship is disturbed by a compassionate annoyance that the story should be as it is, and that the moral he must draw should obey it. In a literature controlled by male authorship and its priorities (which are those of the State, and society) the representation of women is one against which women in their time were unable to complain, or counter-demonstrate with a literature of their own, except, perhaps, in private, and in forms which have not survived. Foreign visitors to Scotland in Dunbar's time commented on the relative independence of women, and how they discussed matters of interest among themselves. Dunbar's 'The Tretis of the Tua Mariit Wemen and the Wedo' is, in fact, an inventive and vigorous example of an anti-feminist strain in the literature of its period – but part of its ingenuity lies in how it leaves you wondering just how anti-feminist it is, or if it is at all. On Midsummer night, the 'mirriest of nichtis', at around midnight, the poet finds himself in an agreeable garden. He speaks of his pleasant privacy in the dew, among birdsong and 'the savour sanative of the suiet flouris'. He sees 'thre gay ladeis sit in ane grene arbeir' and goes on to describe what they're wearing and how they look:

> So glitterit as the gold wer thair glorius gilt tressis,
> Quhill all the gressis did gleme of the glaid hewis;
> Kemmit was thair cleir hair, and curiouslie shed
> Attour thair schulderis doun schyre, schyning full bricht,
> With curches cassin thair abone of kirsp cleir and thin.
> Thair mantillis grein war as the gress that grew in May sessoun,
> Fetrit with thair quhyt fingaris about thair fair sydis.
> Off ferliful fyne favour war thair faceis meik,
> All full of flurist fairheid as flouris in June,
> Quhyt, seimlie, and soft, as the sweet lillies . . .

And these 'fair wlonkes' give it maximum chit-chat while quaffing 'the wicht wyne'; and they speak with absolute candour. One is a widow of a highly sportive disposition, and the other two are married to noblemen. Instead of joining them – never an option in this kind of poem – Dunbar eavesdrops on the frank conversation between the widow and the two women which is on the subjects of marriage and sex. It's an incident of a sort which can still happen. I remember a famous playwright telling me how he'd been taken short and forced to dash to a loo that turned out to be the Ladies. He'd chosen the middle cubicle. He wasn't long seated there when two young women occupied the adjoining cubicles and began talking loudly to each other about men and sex in a manner not far removed from that of the graffiti on the walls, which had already come as a bit of a shock. Slowly, soundlessly, he raised his feet and lowered trousers from the floor so as not to be identified as a man in that forbidden place. For him, it is now a moment commemorating the death of a contemporary if also demotic version of Courtly Love.

To some extent, Dunbar's poem is too, even if the satire is defending – or seems to be – the compromised moral ground in which that ethic was rooted. But its alliterative, ornamented style sets up throughout a contrast with its vernacular swing. The poem is demotic *and* culturally stylized. While this can seem like fun artifice all the way, Dunbar is satirizing marriage from both the points of view of women identified by him as wanton and the style he employs. The widow asks the two ladies about the happiness they've found in marriage, or whether they believe they would have done better had they enjoyed the right to choose. Marriage is then dismissed in the first answer as a source of misery, constraint and frustration. 'We suld have feiris as fresche to fang quhen us likit,/ And gif all larbaris thair leveis quhen thai lak curage.' That is, in suggesting the contentment of the free woman, the first married lady says she should have the right to enjoy young men whenever she feels like it, and bid farewell to impotent ditherers as soon as they get into that state.

Dunbar's invective makes the lady's case unbeatable:

> I have ane wallidrag, ane worme, ane auld wobat carle,
> A waistit walroun, na worth bot wourdis to clatter,
> Ane bumbart, ane dron bee, ane bag full of flewme,
> Ane skabbit skarth, ane scorpioun, ane scutarde behind;
> To see him scart his awin skyn grit scunner I think.
> Quhen kisses me that carybald, than kyndillis all my sorrow;
> As birs of ane brym hair, his berd is als stif,
> But soft and soupill as the silk is his sary lume;
> He may weill to the syn assent, bot sakles is his deidis.

This unsatisfactory sexual state of affairs is countered by the widow's narrative of marital trickery and the high old times she enjoys in her widowhood, and in her extra-marital pranks before the final and instructive demise of her last husband. She 'takes pity' on any man who shows an interest in her – 'pity' being the euphemism in the terminology of courtly love for a woman agreeing to give in. The three women drink and dance the night away; but the clerical poet sits in his bush and watches. He ends by saying:

> Ye auditoris most honorable, that eris has gevin
> Oneto this uncouth aventur quhilk airly me happinnit:
> Of thir thre wantoun wiffis that I haif writtin heir,
> Quhild wald ye waill to your wif, gif ye suld wed one?

Henryson's *Cresseid* is addressed to women; Dunbar's 'Tretis' is directed at 'auditoris most honorable' – men; – but that looks tactical: it reads like a poem written clandestinely for a female as well as a male readership.

Although an anti-feminist satire, Dunbar's poem shows itself to be under thematic stress. The vernacular zest of what he makes his three women say tends to subvert his moral position. Something which critics have rejoiced in as characteristically Scots has entered his writing. It can be summed up in a single line from 'Kynd Kittock', where the husband, who speaks the poem, says of his wife:

Scho wes like a caldrone cruke, cler under kell:

That is, she looked like a malformed cauldron, but with beautiful hair under her headgear. As Professor Kinsley noted in his otherwise prissy edition, the line consists of grotesque realism and a Romance tag. It is a juxtaposition in miniature of G. Gregory Smith's famous summary of the Scottish imagination as one drawn to depict a grinning gargoyle beside a kneeling saint.

Gavin Douglas's translation of the *Aeneid* is a loftier enterprise, but in Book IV, Dido's anguished protestations and Aeneas's dutiful recoil from love, the entire dynamic of the book, result in a momentum that is as impressively domestic as it is impressively classical. It is almost as if Douglas at a level of consciousness other than the one through which he worked identified Scotland as a potential Troy or Tyre, a land vulnerable to total conquest and destruction, a country of possible refugees. The story of Dido and Aeneas is the loftiest in Western literature of an unequal love affair. No doubt it articulates a great deal about male psychology – the power of duty to break the power of love, for example. Implicit, too, at a deep level of consciousness embedded in the cultural code, but easily brought to the surface is, that by instinctive means, earlier writers were even more prone than their successors to accept women as inherently weak and inferior. That this was then re-codified in Reformation Calvinism is part of the tragic dimension of this story. That is, mediaeval notions were perpetuated into early modern and subsequent times, as if the erotic innovations of the Troubadours had never happened, save for the courtly poets of James I's Castalian Band. In Henryson, Dunbar, and Douglas, there seems to have been released moments of restiveness before the established moral wisdom, but a disquietude that was never likely to go all the way with its intuitions.

In a well known remark on this period of Scottish poetry, Edwin Muir claimed:

The Scottish poets followed the tradition of Dunbar, who expressed the exuberance, wildness, and eccentricity of the Middle Ages, not that of Henryson, who inherited the mediaeval completeness and harmony, and had the power to see life whole, without taking refuge in the facetious and the grotesque. Yet Henryson embodies more strikingly than any other poet who has written since the fundamental seriousness, humanity, and strength of the Scottish imagination.

However, Muir is generalizing about a Scottish imagination that by the time of Henryson, Dunbar, and Douglas, had admitted few if any women into the written record.

Even if we accept the established view that the time-span of the Scottish ballads extends from around 1350 to the early or mid-eighteenth century, and if we accept that genuine ballads were not written by individual authors but by a process of composition and transmission in which specific authorship was unimportant, then I think a case can be made for the participation of women in that cultural phenomenon. In what can be regarded as relatively early ballad – 'The Elfin Knight' – the story shows a young woman defend her virginity against a wily, supernatural would-be seducer. As one editor has said of this kind of folk story, 'Ballad maidens, like Oedipus in the paws of the Sphinx, have only mother wit to rely upon'. Dunbar demonstrates convincingly that he could dramatize a widow and two high-born ladies to whom 'mother wit' is far from alien. But he uses it to discredit them, or make them seem unattractive to a reasonable man, or underline just how independent women can be in a society which does not tolerate such behaviour. Their mental adroitness is all in the service of lubricity, clandestine or illicit amours, or wishing for the means to break free of their marriages. 'The Elfin Knight' is about a successful defence of chastity in the face of fairy cunning. It only makes sense if you imagine the poem appealing to women, performed by a woman, and probably written by one before being passed on to others to memorize and modify.

1   The elphin knight sits on yon hill,
     Ba, ba, ba, lilli ba
   He blaws his horn both lowd and shril.
     The wind hath blown my plaid awa

2   He blowes it east, he blowes it west,
   He blowes it where he lyketh best.

3   'I wish that horn were in my kist,
   Yea, and the knight in my armes two.'

4   She had no sooner these words said
   When that the knight came to her bed.

5   'Thou are over young a maid,' quoth he,
    'Married with me thou il wouldst be.'

6   'I have a sister younger than I,
    And she was married yesterday.'

7   'Married with me if thou wouldst be,
    A courtesie thou must do to me.

8   'For thou must shape a sark to me,
    Without any cut or heme,' quoth he.

9   'Thou must shape it [knife]-and-sheerlesse,
    And also sue it needle-threadlesse.'

10 'If that piece of courtesie I do to thee,
    Another thou must do to me.

11 'I have an aiker of good ley-land,
    Which lyeth low by yon sea-strand.

12 'For thou must eare it with thy horn,
    So thou must sow it with thy corn.

13 'And bigg a cart of stone and lyme,
    Robin Readbreast he must trail it hame.

14 'Thou must barn it in a mouse-holl,
    And thrash it into thy shoes' soll.

15 'And thou must winnow it in thy looff,
    And also seck it in thy glove.

16 'For thou must bring it over the sea,
    And thou must bring it dry home to me.

17 'When thou hast gotten thy turns well done,
    Then come to me and get thy sark then.'

18 'I'l not quite my plaid for my life;
    It haps my seven bairns and my wife.'
    The wind shall not blow my plaid awa

19   'My maidenhead I'l then keep still,
      Let the elphin knight do what he will.'
      The wind's not blown my plaid awa

      kist, chest *sark*, shirt *ley*, fallow *eare*, plow
      bigg, build *looff*, palm of the hand *seck*, sack

Contentious and speculative as that point might be – I can no sooner
prove that a ballad like 'The Elfin Knight' was written by a woman than you
can prove that it was composed by a man – there is evidence other than
tone, or appeal, or which sex seems the natural singer of the song, or a
general feminine run of perceptions through it, to support a claim that the
involvement of women in balladry was bigger than is sometimes supposed.
The source of around thirty ballads in the mid-eighteenth century, for
example, was a Mrs Brown of Falkland, who probably rewrote many of
them, and may have composed some on her own account, to say nothing
of how her sources coloured them in their own way. At the turn of the
nineteenth and the present century the poets who made a mark with verse
in Scots, and whose themes and forms bear a distinct resemblance to ballad
poetry, were women, especially Violet Jacob. Singers among the travelling
people of Scotland from whom detective folklorists have collected versions
of ballad words and tunes were largely women. Also, it was James Hogg's
mother who communicated ballads to Sir Walter Scott, and who recorded
her lamentation that by writing them down and publishing them Scott
would kill off the folk tradition. Some of Muriel Spark's novels bear on
balladry, *The Ballad of Peckham Rye*, for instance, and, or so I'd claim, *The
Prime of Miss Jean Brodie* – it's close to 'Marie Hamilton' in its mood and
movement of feeling.
   None of that is especially conclusive. However, what clinches the matter
– for me, at any rate – is the case of *Hardyknute, a Fragment*, which was
published in Edinburgh in 1719. It is a poem of 216 lines arranged in 27
stanzas. Contemporary attitudes look back on it as a forgery, and not even
a good one, for the poem was decked out with old spelling to make it look
like a relic of a hundred-and-fifty or two hundred years before; it's close to
a would-be poetic prank of the sort indulged in later by Chatterton. And, as
David Masson says in an essay on the subject (*Edinburgh Sketches & Memories*, 1892), that is how it was welcomed. No one would be taken in today
– the language is distant from an authentic sixteenth-century Scots idiom.
Those gulled by it, however, included Duncan Forbes of Culloden, later
Lord President, and Sir Gilbert Elliott of Minto, subsequently Lord Justice-
Clerk. Masson suggests that it came into their hands via Lord Binning, who
received a manuscript copy from Sir John Hope Bruce of Kinross (later a

lieutenant-general) who claimed that the original, in a state of disrepair, had been discovered recently in a vault in Dunfermline. Subsequently, the poem was republished in Allan Ramsay's *Evergreen* (1724). By 1740, it appeared in London, *Hardyknute, A Fragment; being the first Canto of an Epick Poem: with general remarks and notes.* And it was still thought to be of not later than the sixteenth century. 'There is a grandeur, a majesty of sentiment, diffused through the whole,' says the nameless editor, 'a true sublime, which nothing can surpass.' Next stop Bishop Percy's *Reliques of Ancient English Poetry* in 1765, and in subsequent editions in 1767, 1775, and 1794, gathering more and more scholarly notes along the way. Thomas Gray rated it highly; and so did Thomas Warton – 'a noble poem', he called it. 'It was the first poem I ever learnt, the last I shall ever forget,' said Sir Walter Scott, who would have known from Percy's edition of 1767 the suspicion, conveyed to Percy by Lord Hailes (who, just conceivably, wrote the famous ballad 'Edward', or cribbed it) that, as Masson puts it, *Hardyknute* 'was substantially the composition of a Scottish lady, who had died in 1727 . . .' Note that the woman in question was not mentioned by name. She was Elizabeth Halket, born in 1677, a daughter of Sir Charles Halket of Pitfirran, and who married Sir Henry Wardlaw of Pitreavie in 1696. Her work has had to contest the issue with F. J. Child, in his great collection of the Ballads – 'tiresome and affected', he called it, and 'of slight account'. His criticism is probably true as far as it goes; but it avoids the issue of feminine involvement in balladry or the direction in which Lady Wardlaw, or Mrs Brown of Falkland, ought to take us.

Not only was Lady Wardlaw the author of *Hardyknute*, but there is at least the possibility that she, or others, had a hand in some of the best known ballad poems first presented by Percy or in later collections by Herd (1769), Scott (1802) and Jamieson (1806), Motherwell, and Kirkpatrick Sharpe. Among them are 'Sir Patrick Spens', 'The Jew's Daughter', 'Marie Hamilton', 'The Gay Goss Hawk' and 'Sweet William's Ghost'. That it *is* a possibility, and might even be stronger than that, is suggested by the verse of *Hardyknute* itself, which we know (at least, more or less) to be by Lady Wardlaw. Here are the opening stanzas of the poem:

> Stately stept he east the wa'
>   And stately stept he west;
> Full seventy years he now had seen,
>   With scarce seven years of rest.
> He lived when Britons' breach of faith
>   Wrocht Scotland mickle wae;
> And aye his sword tauld, to their cost,
>   He was their deadly fae.

High on a hill his castle stood,
  With halls and tower a-hicht,
And guidly chambers fair to see,
  Whare he lodged mony a knicht.
His dame, sae peerless ance and fair,
  For chaste and beauty deemed,
Nae marrow had in a' the land,
  Save Eleanour the Queen.

Full thirteen sons to him she bare,
  All men of valour stout;
In bluidy fecht with sword in hand
  Nine lost their lives bot doubt:
Four yet remain; lang may they live
  To stand by liege and land!
High was their fame, high was their micht,
  And high was their command.

Great love they bare to Fairly fair,
  Their sister saft and dear:
Her girdle shawed her middle jimp,
  And gowden glist her hair.
What waefu' wae her beauty bred,
  Waefu' to young and auld;
Waefu', I trow, to kith and kin,
  As story ever tauld!

Bearing in mind William Hamilton of Bangour's 'The Braes of Yarrow', which is an emotional obbligato on the authentically old ballad 'The Dowie Dens O Yarrow', then another likelihood is that Lady Wardlaw (but not in *Hardyknute*) and others drew from older sources still held in the memory of women and men in their localities. Hamilton, though, like Lady Wardlaw, was well connected, and aristocratic. Right from the beginning of what could be termed a 'ballad revival' in Scotland, a revivification of popular poetry, major revivalists did not stem from the folk but from higher echelons of society. Anna Gordon, or Mrs Brown of Falkland, was not of humble birth, either, although, like others, in close proximity to women, and men, for whom the oral poetic tradition was still – evidently – a living force. One consequence of Lady Wardlaw's station in life was anonymity. Masson writes that it was 'less a desire for mystification than an amiable shrinking from publicity, dislike of being talked of as a literary lady'. This, he says:

was a feeling which the ungenerous mankind of the last century, – husbands, brothers, uncles, and brothers-in-law, – thought it proper to foster in any feminine person of whose literary accomplishments they were privately proud.

And, as well as proud, they were not beyond a chuckle at the mystification *they* perpetrated, and of which Lady Wardlaw was probably blameless. The episode looks more shabby than Masson admits, although he continues by saying that an imposed anonymity, or silence, 'affected the careers of not a few later Scottish women of genius in the same century, and even through part of our own'.

In retrospect, guided, that is, by the critical priorities of our own time, the submergence of Lady Wardlaw (and, later, Lady Nairne) seems of greater significance than the workings of social convention. Subsequent women writers have had too few highlighted female predecessors to look back on. Lady John Scott, for example, wrote 'Annie Laurie', one of the most famous of Scottish songs, and there were other women active in writing lyrics throughout the eighteenth and nineteenth centuries. Carolina Oliphant (b. 1766), later Lady Nairne, was among the best; but her career is remarkable for the anonymity and seclusion which she imposed on it. For almost fifty years of her lifetime men and women were singing her songs without knowing who wrote them, while she mixed in a society which included Sir Walter Scott, and other luminaries. It seems probable that her husband knew nothing of her authorship, either. Reticence, if it is a virtue, was taken by Lady Nairne to an elevation that transformed anonymity into an art in its own right. It was only a year after her death in 1846 that she became known as the writer of songs like 'Wi' a hundred pipers . . .', 'The Laird o' Cockpen', 'John Tod', 'Caller Herrin'' and 'The Land o' the Leal'. Aristocratic as she was, of a Jacobite family, Lady Nairne drew her songs from a reservoir of popular Scottish feelings and cadences. The first verse of 'The Land o' the Leal' reads:

> I'm wearin' awa, Jean,
> Like snaw-wreaths in thaw, Jean,
> I'm wearin' awa
>   To the land o' the leal.
> There's nae sorrow there, Jean;
> There's nae cauld nor care, Jean;
> The day is aye fair
>   In the land o' the leal.

What Lady Nairne wrote was 'I'm wearin' awa', *John*'. Interestingly, instead of a dying woman (which is more common in Scottish poetry) by popular, probably male consensus, the poem's gender was turned around. Written apparently in 1796, for years it was believed that the song must have been penned by the dying Robert Burns. Perhaps that manly error encouraged the elision of 'he' into 'she'.

Although sentimental in the manner of many Scottish songs, 'The Land o' the Leal', like most of Lady Nairne's lyrics, is accomplished and marked with a touch of genius for the sustaining of an indigenous mode of poetry and melody. What it can't compare with are songs by Burns of the order of 'Mary Morison' and 'John Anderson my Jo', among many others, but these two especially. As everyone knows, 'John Anderson' is a politer, slightly sentimentalized version of an older song. While the woman's voice in Burns's version is convincing, the original's candour is superior, and it could be less than far-fetched to suppose its original author was a woman. It doesn't make much sense sung by a man. But the question must be – why did a man possess, or re-possess, a song sung by a woman and probably composed by a woman? I believe the answer to be 'cultural apology'.

> John Anderson, my jo, John
>   When first that ye began,
> Ye had as good a tail-tree,
>   As ony ither man;
> But now its waxen wan, John,
>   And wrinkles to and fro'
> I've twa gae-ups for ae gae-down,
>   John Anderson, my jo.

Scottish songs of the eighteenth-century are densely populated with real or fictitious women, and women were among their authors. Just as it is misleading to see balladry and song as the products of a genderless people's commonweath, so is it a calculated act of gender cleansing to see the song culture of the eighteenth century and later as essentially male.

Scotland, like the Muse, is a feminine term and Idea. Among the more obvious examples are Dame Scotia in *The Complaynt of Scotland*, Scota in Ross's *Helenore*, Burns's more local Muse, Coila, in *The Vision*, and perhaps also Kilmeny in James Hogg's magnificent poem of magical nationalism and lyrical affront in which Kilmeny spectates on the past and present predicaments of Scotland. It is an imaginative embodiment that leads to Chris Caledonia in Grassic Gibbon's novel. A more demotic, boozy version can be witnessed in Sydney Goodsir Smith's 'Kynd Kittock's Land' or Eric Linklater's story based on the same poem by William Dunbar. Scotia can be dignified, proud, and lovely; she can be Queen Margaret, Mary, Queen of Scots, all the women in the songs and all the women who ever wrote them, sang them or heard them. She can be Kate, Mrs Tam o' Shanter, 'Gathering her brows like gathering storm,/ Nursing her wrath to keep it warm', or the nimble daemon Nannie in hot pursuit of the terrified drunkard mounted on his mare. She can be anything you like. Patriarchal, or man-centred, as the contract between the sexes in Scotland was for so long, there are times when the pathos of poetry and fiction make you feel that a longing for matriarchy is trying to break through. Literary and actual attitudes to women may not always be respectable by contemporary standards, but there is a lot about women in Scottish writing by its predominantly male authorship.

A glance at some of Sir Walter Scott's heroines and other female characters might illustrate that point. Diana Vernon in *Rob Roy* is one of his most remarkable characters altogether. When Francis Osbaldistone, who narrates the story, first meets her, he writes:

> It was a young lady, the loveliness of whose very striking features was enhanced by the animation of the chase and the glow of the exercise, mounted on a beautiful horse, jet black, unless where he was flecked by spots of the snow-white foam which embossed his bridle. She wore, what was then unusual, a coat, vest, and hat, resembling those of a man, which fashion has since called a riding habit.

Scott was obsessed with women in masculine riding gear. In *Redgauntlet*, Darsie Latimer is obliged to assume disguise as a woman. He speaks in his own person, describing what he is to wear:

> A skirt, or upper-petticoat of camlet, like those worn by country-ladies of moderate rank when on horseback, with such a riding-mask as they frequently use on journeys to preserve their eyes and complexion from the sun and dust, and sometimes, it is suspected, to enable them to play off a little coquetry. From the gayer mode of employing the mask, however, I suspect I shall be precluded; for instead of being only pasteboard, covered with black velvet, I observe with anxiety that mine is thickened with a plate of steel, which, like Quixote's visor, serves to render it more strong and durable.

Whether fetishistic or amusing might depend on individual taste, innocence, or lack of it; but that detail 'upper-petticoat of camlet' reminds me of a remark by the late Marganita Laski when reviewing a novel of A. N. Wilson's set in the Victorian period. Mr Wilson mentioned someone's 'trowser' (spelling it like that) which, Ms Laski claimed, was pornographic in the intimacy with which it laid claim to the reader's attention.

About a hundred pages later Scott returns to Darsie, this time the narrator being the omnipotent novelist.

The metamorphosis was complete; for the fair reader must be informed that in those rude times, the ladies, when they honoured the masculine dress by assuming any part of it, wore just such hats, coats, and waistcoats, as the male animals themselves made use of, and had no notion of the elegant compromise betwixt male and female attire, which has now acquired, *par excellence*, the name of a *habit*. Trolloping things our mothers must have looked, with long square-cut coats, lacking collars, and with waistcoats splendidly supplied with a length of pocket, which hung far downwards from the middle. But then they had some advantage from the splendid colours, lace, and gay embroidery, which masculine attire then exhibited; and, as happens in many similar instances, the finery of the materials made amends for the want of symmetry and grace of form in the garments themselves. But this is a digression.

How, I wonder, would Scott have reacted to jodhpurs?

As well as sexually alluring, Diana Vernon in *Rob Roy* is spirited and discontent with the limitations placed on her by being a woman. 'Forsake the faith of my gallant fathers!' she exclaims. 'I would as soon, were I a man, forsake their banner when the tide of battle pressed hardest against it, and turn, like a hireling recreant, to join the victorious enemy.'

She'd sooner wear military headgear than have long hair tied up with hair-combs. But she is also fiercely bookish:

'And what are those studies, if I may presume to ask?'
'Indeed, you may, without the least fear of seeing my forefinger raised to my chin. Science and history are my principal favourites; but I also study poetry and the classics.'
'And the classics? Do you read them in the original?'
'Unquestionably.'

Indeed, as well as Latin and Greek, Diana reads most of the languages of modern Europe. A vivid passage of dialogue then underlines that there is nothing pedantic about her attainments.

'I assure you that there has been some pains taken in my education, although I can neither sew a tucker, nor work cross-stitch, nor make a pudding, nor – as the vicar's fat wife, with as much truth as elegance, good-will, and politeness, was pleased to say in my behalf – do any other useful thing in the varsal world.'

Not unsurprisingly, Diana is aware of how men (and women) resent her scholarship, her well-informed mind, as well as her forthrightness and her gifts as a horsewoman, dead shot, and mimic. Why? Because she is also beautiful, and, for Scott, her bookishness, glamour and athleticism, are all part of her sexiness. As well as providing the foundations of the lethal and gallant chivalry of the Confederacy, as Mark Twain bewailed, Scott could also have cast the mould from which Calamity Jane was poured.

Powerful and fascinating as she is, it seems never to have dawned on Scott that his creation invited generalizing on the subject of women. Diana is a *heroine* and, therefore, exceptional, as well as contained by the mental and moral boundaries of Scott's fictitious world. Whatever reality he drew her from is allowed to recede into a background too distant even to see let alone relate her to it. Fiction is allowed to triumph over social history at the same time as it expresses political history.

In *Redgauntlet*, however, Lilias, or Green Mantle, emerges from a reality, or a memory of one, which can be identified. As a young man Scott fancied himself in love with Williamina, the daughter of Sir John Stuart-Belsches of Fettercairn. In his biography, John Buchan drew attention to an extant portrait of Williamina, and pointed to

> composed features, large blue eyes, dark brown ringlets and a complexion of cream and roses.

He writes, too, that in his youth Williamina was toasted by Scott's friends as The Lady of the Green Mantle. When you bear in mind the episode of Green Breeks recounted by Scott in his own words in Lockhart's *Life*, the feminized male name – Williamina – is provocative when associated with the colour green. It's as if Scott searched for his own Forest of Arden in which sexual transformation and liberty were feasible.

When Alan Fairford first encounters Lilias, this is how he reports the event to his friend Darsie:

> My visitor was undeniably a lady, and probably considerably above the ordinary rank – very modest, too, judging from the mixture of grace and timidity with which she moved, and at my entreaty sat down. Her dress was, I should suppose, both handsome and fashionable; but it was much concealed by a walking-cloak of green silk, fancifully embroidered; in which, though heavy for the season, her person was enveloped, and which, moreover, was furnished with a hood . . . a clasp of gold, ornamented with a sapphire, closed the envious mantle under the incognita's throat, and the cursed hood concealed entirely the upper part of the face.

Witnessed in that tantalizing passage is the not uncommon event of a fictitious character drawn from real memory in terms which express a drama of regret as well as fondness. Partial concealment of the woman's face, the jewellery, the occasion in an *act* of fiction when the *real* Green Mantle becomes the elusive property of imaginative *re*-creation, evinces the hide-and-seek of the fiction-making imagination itself when it deals with such psychologically risky material. Regret, fondness, and imagination, can work together to create an illusory, fictitious possession, the spurious satisfaction of writing a real life in terms of the author's own. That is not a male prerogative. Think of Heathcliff. It is sexual fantasy, which is human, common to both sexes, if also different in each.

That Green Mantle, or Lilias Redgauntlet, is a female character created by male sexual fantasy becomes clearer later in the story. Darsie describes Lilias in these terms:

> . . . the slight derangement of the beautiful brown locks which escaped in natural ringlets from under her riding-hat, with the bloom which exercise had brought into her cheek, made her even more than usually fascinating.

That description in close-up – it is very specific, but also in soft focus – is shot through with sexual desire – Scott's and Darsie's. Cunningly, but perhaps for too long to be entirely credible, Scott is withholding crucial information. It's done not just to tease the reader, but thrill Scott. Lilias begins:

> 'Goodness – gratitude! – O Darsie! should these be the phrases between you and me? – Alas! I am too sure you are displeased with me, though I cannot even guess on what account. Perhaps you think I have been too free in venturing upon my visit to your friend. But then remember, it was in your behalf, and that I knew no better way to put you on your guard against the misfortune and restraint which you have been subjected to, and are still enduring.'
>
> 'Dear Lady' – said Darsie, rallying his recollection, and suspicious of some error in apprehension, – a suspicion which his mode of address seemed at once to communicate to Lilias, for she interrupted him, –
>
> '*Lady*! dear lady! – For whom, or for what, do you take me, that you address me so formally?'
>
> Had the question been asked in that enchanted hall in Fairyland, where all interrogations must be answered with absolute sincerity, Darsie had certainly replied, that he took her for the most frank-hearted and ultra-liberal lass that had ever lived since Mother Eve ate the pippin without paring. But as he was still on middle-earth, and

free to avail himself of a little polite deceit, he barely answered, that he believed he had the honour of speaking to the niece of Mr Redgauntlet.

'Surely,' she replied; 'but were it not as easy for you to have said, to your own only sister?'

Darsie started in his saddle, as if he had received a pistol-shot.

'My sister!' he exclaimed.

Remember – he's still in his riding-skirt, riding side-saddle.

Chekhov believed that it was a cardinal sin to humiliate a character – which is what Scott does to both Darsie and Green Mantle/Lilias Redgauntlet while playing on Darsie's embarrassment at having subjected to sexual contemplation the young woman who turns out to be his sister. This tactic, this sporting with taboo, makes it inevitable that Alan Fairford will win Lilias – and Scott himself is the model for Alan. Or to be straightforward about it, Alan/Scott wins Lilias/Williamina, and the regrets of reality are turned into the delights of fiction. Lilias, however, is 'used' in another way, too. (But Scott is also 'using' himself.) As niece and daughter of a Jacobite family, seen from the beginning as competent, hooded, mysterious, forbidden, as well as beautiful, her 'new life' can be released only after her Jacobite pedigree can be countermanded and her uncle sent off into exile with the Pretender. In Scott's terms, Lilias, Darsie and Alan are representatives of national redemption from the glamorous but fated entrapments of Jacobitism. They are an optimistic younger generation, poised before happiness and the continued opportunities of the Union. Scott intermingles the erotic with the political, a fact which ought to complicate our reading of him, especially as, with Rebecca in *Ivanhoe*, he blends the erotic with the historical. But if Lilias seems at times of crucial importance to the book, its structure devalues her fictional prestige. Narrative voices in the shape of Darsie, Alan, and an authorial narrator, as well as the counterpoint provided by 'Wandering Willie's Tale', exclude the possibility of Lilias as a point of view. Author, Darsie, Alan, and the reader, have points of view on Lilias Redgauntlet; Lilias does not in the novel exert a point of view of her own except through the extent to which Scott succeeds in realizing her as a character – and it is that very success which leads the modern reader to distrust the missing structural ingredient as a symptom of Scott's ingrained inhibition. He can take a woman character only so far, and always within either his own narrative voice, or that of another male protagonist, or the female character's dialogue, but not a female character's narrative.

Part of Scott's withholding on this issue is dictated by the times in which he lived and the existence of barriers which were difficult to break even in fiction. Implicated also, and perhaps with equivalent force, is Scott's determination to reflect significant Scottish history mediated through moments of high, transitional drama. *The Heart of Midlothian* is not a clear exception, but the tension and suspense in scenes between Effie Deans and her sister Jeanie feminize action and psychology at least at the level of encounter. From the perspective of this subject, it can hardly be avoided – the story involves a parricide in which both son and father are unwitting, and the mother – Effie Deans – is in ignorance. By this point the fiction begins to reach out to the legendary and the mythical. A bold, courageous and instinctive embrace of the national and the populist is initiated, but the novel cannot bear it – Effie Deans' son is a figure of inverted Romance: for him, there is no inheritance or recognition, only the possibility that he might have survived among an American Indian tribe, as one of them. Energy is increased in *The Heart of Midlothian* through the vernacular of the characters who really matter – their Scots idiom dredges up from Scott's imaginative powers aboriginal authenticity as well as an incentive to *try* to live by its veracity and impetus. In *The Heart of Midlothian* his heroines are Wordsworthian rather than Byronic or Romantic Scottesque sexual statuary. Madge Wildfire, for instance, comes straight from an allegedly original eccentric who was known as Feckless Fannie, a shepherdess and lunatic – the 'original' could be pure cod for all I know, but in Scott's note on the subject it reads like a story which Wordsworth could have cast in desolating and pathetic verse.

Whether as saints (Scott's fated Lucy Ashton in *The Bride of Lammermoor*, for example), equestrian intellectuals, sinners (Dunbar's widow and two married women), saintly sinners (Henryson's Cresseid), heroines exuding allure on author and male reader, the structure of the male representation of women in Scottish literature is complicated but by and large categorizable. Modern literature is not all that different in the range of examples it offers. It is more self-aware, and it is that lacerating self-consciousness which is examined by, for example, Alasdair Gray but not, or not yet, by James Kelman or William McIlvanney. In very general terms, male Scottish writers still seem trapped by inherited psychologies. Instead of the psycho-sexual drama exhibited by Sir Walter Scott, a Romanticist sexual theatre of the imagination, they portray a more cultural masculinity.

Within the precepts of that code literature is a male-sanctioned activity among those for whom it is important. But among those for whom it is not, it is an alternative system of values, one which breaks the code. In a country like Scotland where social class is visibly divisive, literature as a route into a more benevolent structure of values is an important issue, related as it is to questions of language and identity as well as gender and political nationalism. What, then, is the position of women in Scottish literature? One answer can be found in an essay by a recent critic, Margery Metzstein. She goes so far as to state that the term 'Scottish writer' constructs an identity which is not applicable to women writers who are Scottish.

It is easy to understand why such an exclusive decision is felt necessary. It simply reflects a fact. Under-represented in terms of numbers of female participants, neglected or patronized when they write and publish, misrepresented as saints, trollops, the 'strong woman', the 'victim', as termagant, or slattern, as long-suffering mum, women writers in Scotland need only survey the depressing canon before concluding that its rejection could be enabling and creative. But that decision includes the germ of cultural tragedy. Poetry, fiction and drama have their moods of prohibition and repudiation, but it is rare that any one of them should reject itself. That, however, is the destructive possibility on offer when a culture overrates its nationalism at the expense of curative and benign human relationships.

There is a moment in J. MacDougall Hay's grim but powerful novel *Gillespie* when the principal character finds a placard nailed to his door. It reads:

THIS HOUSE IS DEAD.
IT HAS BEEN MURDERED.
IT IS BURIED IN THE GRAVE OF A WOMAN'S HEART.

Those of us who live in the house of literature should not have to open its door to collect the milk and newspapers and find that message pinned to it.

University of St Andrews

MARILYN REIZBAUM

Not a crying game
The Feminist Appeal: Nationalism, Feminism and the Contemporary Literatures of Scotland and Ireland

I

The double entendre that is the title of this talk is at the very heart of what I perhaps loosely, but hopefully call a relationship between feminism and nationalism in contemporary Scotland and Ireland. Feminism's recent appeal in the sense of exhortation to the national or nationalist establishments in these countries has been manifold; in response, these establishments almost always rewrite this appeal, not unintentionally, as *feminine* – radical ravings or snivelling entreaties, which are repellent and/or pathetic, or maybe cute, but most pointedly, distracting from a subsumptive nationalist imperative, and therefore 'worthy' of dismissal or benevolent correction. And while such apprehensions of feminism seek to demean and to (re)place women into their historical positions as personifications of the national – the Kathleen ni Houlihans, Shan Van Vochts, the virgin brides – these two seemingly disparate notions of appeal (feminist and feminine) may be conflated. That is, what has been historically construed as feminine is precisely what radically threatens and is pathologically rejected by the 'hard men' of nationalism; the 'appeal' is too reminiscent of historical representations of the ab/subject people as feminine, womanish, where a disempowerment of a culture becomes an emasculation. This is a representation of the nation appropriated by cultural nationalism and put back 'where it belongs', onto the sacrificing woman who becomes the emblematic prop.[1] I'm thinking here of the Dark Rosaleens of James Clarence Mangan or Hugh MacDiarmid's thistle bride, for example. For whatever ambiguities they may contain as representations, as emblems they resonate unambiguously. The nationalist impulse to mirror the colonizer's (albeit mythic) standard of strength and unity, to be 'hardmen' – this being the qualifying description, in all of its resonant glory, of the IRA soldier – ironically underlies the need to dismiss/dominate the feminine. For nationalisms in both the Scottish and Irish contexts, gender provides not only an analogic category for national definition, they are intricately and intertextually bound within a constellation of notions about identity and belonging. In this light, the feminist appeal becomes a bind, more than a dismissible cliché defined by the 'impotency' of the feminine. It becomes sex appeal, where female desire and longing for possession of place are translated into dangerous acts of betrayal. Its agents tempt men away from their proper devotions; they are seductresses who seek to unman, to bring the nation to its knees. They are Eves, Circes, Cleopatras, possibly Maeves. Feminism's oppositional stance from within these approximately postcolonial cultures challenges the unity and integrity that are deemed necessary to repel the oppositional force from without. Efforts to deflect the feminist (sex) appeal become more ferocious until feminism is consistently construed as code for lesbianism, as traitorous to the national cause and to sex itself. With this potential for the confusion of roles, the mirror of male potency that stands between colonial and colonizer appears two-way: women might be hard men; men can be feminine or even national(ist) props.

II

At the conclusion of Neil Jordan's compelling film, *The Crying Game*, the transvestite Dil, whose pronoun reference is 'she' throughout the film, is sitting across from Fergus, separated from him by a glass cage in the prison where he is serving time for the murder of his former IRA accomplice and lover, Jude; it is Dil, in fact, who shot Jude in a double act of revenge and protection. Jude had come to avenge betrayal by Fergus, IRA style, though for which act of betrayal is unclear – or perhaps doubly clear. A bit like Yeats' 'Twilight' Fergus, this Fergus was meant to redeem himself for a previous transgression through a suicide mission; instead he has been literally tied up with and by the 'wee black chick,' as Jude refers to Dil, whom Jude understands Fergus prefers over her. Jude is the hard woman, keeper of the faith, and name-sake of the saint of lost causes; she was the lure that lead to the death of Jody, the black English soldier who is the point person for this whole scenario; he was Dil's actual lover, and Fergus' imaginary one, I would argue, who is, in any case, a spectre of loss, betrayal and revenge for Fergus. It is visiting day at the prison, and Dil arrives along with the 'other' wives. In wondering aloud why Fergus, her hero, has thus sacrificed for her, she recites the first three telling words of that old nugget, '*no greater love* hath man than to lay down his life for his friend'; his reply to her query about the reason for his sacrifice is that it's in his nature, recalling the fable about the scorpion and the frog that Jody tells Fergus before he dies:

JODY: Scorpion wants to cross a river, but he can't swim. Goes to the frog, who can, and asks for a ride. Frog says, 'If I give you a ride on my back, you'll go and sting me.' Scorpion replies, 'It would not be in my interest to sting you since as I'll be on your back we both would drown.' Frog thinks about this logic for a while and accepts the deal. Takes the scorpion on this back. Braves the waters. Halfway over feels a burning spear in his side and realizes the scorpion has stung him after all. And as they both sink beneath the waves the frog cries out, 'why did you sting me, Mr Scorpion, for now we both will drown?' Scorpion replies, 'I can't help it, it's in my nature.' (Jordan, 196).

Those last lines and images resonate all over the place: they remind of the first scenes of the film where Fergus guards Jody at the IRA hideout, where, you might say, one casualty/prisoner of nationalism guards another, expressed here at the conclusion in yet another configuration as prisoners of love; where the same story is told with the same enigmatic lesson about nature; where clichés about nation and nature align. It is not clear from Jody's first telling what the import of his fable is, since Fergus seems to fit neither category of the scorpion or the frog. What human story does this tell? There is a kind of unthinking equation possible between the frog and Fergus, who has been in such a reading generous at his own expense. But is the frog's act heroic, or does it mimic a certain [feminine] projection of the nationalist's self sacrifice, where illusions of altruism must be maintained at all cost? And are these the same thing? Heroism in these terms is illusory. The frog may be seen as either denying what every frog should know – the nature of a scorpion – or being duped by the scorpion's logic that belies that nature, just as Fergus is either fooled by or denies Dil's nature, or his own. (Dil at one point pleads, 'I can't help what I am.' Jordan, p. 257.) And whom does the scorpion represent, making a beguiling appeal, all the while knowing what is his nature? It's not clear whether to read this as a wish to deny nature or to rehearse it. 'No greater love,' presented so elliptically in relation to a question about Fergus' problematic heroism, reminds of *Dulce et decorum est pro patria mori*, where country stands in for friend. Jordan's film displaces country from the phrase, and complicates its place in the sentiment, arguing that its inclusion is a historical displacement, in which the crying game is made into the patriot's game. And if nation is here displaced, 'friend' is at the very least ambiguous.[2]

III

I begin here not only because I am interested in this film's appeal, in, at least, every sense I have laid out at the start of this presentation, but because I see this recent film as a cultural product of the ongoing and recently enlivened debate between nationalism (both cultural and political) and feminism in Ireland. The heat has been generated lately by the furore surrounding the publication of the *Field Day Anthology of Irish Writing*, which sought, by its own proclamation, to jostle and dislodge the chronicles and myths of the history of colonization of Ireland by revealing its national betrayals from within; it does so by including the documents of both sides and thereby extending those sides into more than two oppositional forces. But it repeats these histories and its betrayals when it neither observes the 'colonization' of women by the literary establishments nor seeks to correct that by significantly including work by women in a compendium that is meant to be comprehensively representative of Irish letters. This last critique has been made by Eavan Boland who is well-known inside and, increasingly, outside of Ireland.[3] Her work, both as poet and critic, has been instrumental in forging a dialogue between forces particularly in Ireland, challenging the literary establishments, and the poetics which are sanctioned by them. I will return to her in a moment. I believe that a writer like Neil Jordan, whose work as writer and filmmaker before this has approached but not successfully evinced an understanding of the intertextuality of gender and nationality, in 'The Crying Game' reflects the widening impact of efforts by Boland and other Irish women writers, who I'll name and discuss below, of filmmaker Pat Murphy, who made the debate visible in her movie, 'Maeve,' of the recent director of the Abbey theatre, Garry Hynes, who was before that the director of the innovative Druid Theatre based in Galway, and in both cases known for her provocative recastings of the national tradition (I'm thinking in particular of her 1991 production of O'Casey's *The Plough and the Stars*, where both woman's resistance to and man's fear of national conflict are legitimized, where 'hard men' are played by ambiguously gendered figures, who appear literally neutered by the conflict, and where the history of colonial violence is not dismissed in the course of the production's critique of the national response, but literally drapes, in the form of an enormous Union Jack, the stage and all that is acted out there). I also want to mention here the enormous impact of the position and politics of a Mary Robinson (President of Ireland), as symbol and player, and the, for some, surprising impact of the maelstrom of objections to the *Field Day Anthology*'s acts of omission, rather than of, as its all male editors hoped, what it has included.

My work in this area began with the genre of poetry, not only because it was most prevalent, most celebrated, particularly in Ireland, but because it is women poets in each place who have been most prominent in articulating a case for women writers and for the intersections between nationalism and feminism, gender and nationhood, national and sexual definition. I believe that the work of writers like Boland, Medbh McGuckian, Nuala Ni Dhomnaill, Mary Dorcey, Rita Ann Higgins, Paula Meehan, who are the next generation in Ireland, and Liz Lochhead, Carol Ann Duffy, Dylis Rose,

Sheena Blackhall, and Jackie Kay in Scotland, makes significant contributions to the force field of this debate outside this genre and those cultures. Though they themselves may be invisible to those who encounter their popular progeny, such as Jordan's 'The Crying Game,' Frank McGuinness' 'Someone Who'll Watch Over Me,' even some of Scottish film director Bill Forsyth's work ('Gregory's Girl,' 'Local Hero'), the music of the Proclaimers, Scottish brothers compared to Simon and Garfunkel by *Rolling Stone*, some of Brian Friel's plays, in particular, *Translations* (rather than the more popular *Dancing at Lughnasa*, which I believe romanticizes women more or less in keeping with an Irish literary tradition of such emblematizations, while the former makes the connections between gender and language as complex categories of national definitions). These popular texts are perhaps tellingly all produced by men; but if we set aside gender for a moment in favour of an observation about genre, we might consider that while Boland's work has come into prominent focus in America and elsewhere, it will not, in part by virtue of the genre, have the 'play' that these others do.

In her culturally explosive pamphlet, *A Kind of Scar: The Woman Poet in a National Tradition*, a 1989 Attic Press (woman's press) publication that collects from several essays Boland has written over the last ten years, Boland claims that her exhortations to the Irish literary establishment for their persistent exclusions of women have been, in effect, not so much a critique of nationalism as of a national tradition defined by it. That is, she has always understood and sympathized with the Irish struggle for definition, seeing within it an analogue for the struggles of women against dispossession, though she shuns the literary expressions of these relations in which women, as she says, are the objects rather than the subjects of poetry. In her own poetry as in her critical essays, she has theorized about the way in which she was unconsciously enlisted by those traditions while at once excluded by them as either author or subject. Her critique becomes a tacit criticism of nationalism as it has been realized and promoted in Ireland, as it is sometimes of feminism when the analogue between gender and nation is expressed problematically under the rubric of essentialism.[4] She wrestles with what should be the relationship between a concept of aesthetic value in poetry and the reclamation of, at least, a literary place for women. She has rejected the separatist position which maintains that one cannot reclaim what was never owned, while struggling with the notion of literary inheritance – an ancestral line and language. The title of her pamphlet, *A Kind of Scar*, comes from the poem 'Mise Eire' ('I am Ireland'), where woman as emblem is reconstituted as a lived-life and witness, as Boland would put it; in it, language becomes one site of violent change. Both the woman and the language are emblems of an irretrievable past, not an idealized one. Acts of reclamation for Boland are never wholesale.

Boland's work has evolved as has that of Scottish poet and playwright, Liz Lochhead, from a place in the early work which imagines and constructs what Lochhead calls 'my country of gender,' to a realm like that of her play, *Mary Queen of Scots Got Her head Chopped Off*, where the nation is addressed – even re-dressed.[5] Their work reflects, even anticipates, I would argue, what is the present stage of the polemics around nationhood: their re-dressings are cross-dressings, or border-crossings as Marge Garber, among others, terms these interactions between nationalisms and sexualities.[6] The concept of hybridization, crucial to the present critiques of postcoloniality and nationalism, aligns with the figure of the transvestite, onto which is troped, Garber explains, the 'category crisis' of nationalism and sexuality. If we look, we see this trope and these crises everywhere,[7] most prominently, of course, in *The Crying Game*, where nation and race are signifiers of male impotency in symbolic and literal ways. But instead of hybridization representing as it has traditionally the inadequacy of culture to maintain an integrity – a cultural and/or racial purity – something altogether different is proposed through the sexual analogue of male impotency (Fergus', Dil's), something out of the groove or rut of the nationalisms and sexualities that politically govern the cultural and geographical places of these characters – a new dress or re-mantle.

There is of course much to be said here with regard to the questions that arise from such dramatizations – the seeming erasure of women in much transvestite literature, or the erasure of the history of colonial violence that may be occasioned by such border crossings.[8] I want to end, however, with more about Scotland, else I too much contribute even here to its general underrepresentation and mistreatment. One might wonder how these two cultures might be considered together in these terms, especially given Scotland's Calvinist dissociation from Ireland, as it were, and its cooptation by the so-called United Kingdom into so much violence against and in Ireland, the spectre of which is still very palpable there. Without explaining here what I see as the comparable histories of these for-the-most- part Celtic peoples, especially in their historical relation to England, I will once again use Jordan's text, which, in fact, points to Scotland's border crossing with Ireland: Fergus identifies himself as Jimmy – every Scotsman – once he has decided that this Celt is from Scotland (all Celts are alike). And the principle happily applies when Dil asks if Jude 'is from Scotland too.' 'You could say that,' Fergus replies (Jordan, p. 249). You could.[9]

By identifying himself as a Scot, Fergus is 'skirting' the issue in a way that produces a double entendre of identity; he is pretending to be something he's not by laying claim to something he *would* be. He might have been more identifiable, more distinguishable if he had literally rather than figuratively skirted the issue – by wearing a skirt. Accordingly, I will end with the image of the kilted Scotsman, that product, in part, a kind of spectre of English construction; the clan system is a refashioned, if you will, modern codification of the Scottish clan system, evidence of the English fetishisation of the skirt, the projection, perhaps the idealization of the nation through the feminization of the subject people.[10] But in the same way that Dil's skirt seems to both obscure and reveal her sexuality, so too, like Fergus putting on that identity (makes her something (s)he's not, makes her what she is), the kilt has become an emblem of a two-way street, like the two-way mirror of male potency, like the mantle of Irena that mystifies. The feminine appeal becomes the feminist appeal in as much as the fetishization of the skirt reveals what, as the cliché goes, every observer of the kilt wishes to 'know' – what is underneath!

Bowdoin College, Brunswick, Maine

1   For a discussion of this phenomenon in Irish letters, see, for example, Eavan Boland's *A Kind of Scar: The Woman Poet in a National Tradition* (Dublin: Attic Press Pamphlet, 1989); David Cairns and Shaun Richards, *Writing Ireland: Colonialism, nationalism and culture* (Manchester University Press, 1988); Gerardine Meaney, *Sex and nation: women in Irish culture and politics* (Dublin: Attic Press, 1991); and my 'Canonical Double Cross: Scottish and Irish Woman's Writing,' in *Decolonizing Tradition: New Views of Twentieth-Century British Literary Canons*, ed. Karen Lawrence (Urbana & Chicago: University of Illinois Press, 1992).

2   In Section XII of Seamus Heaney's *Station Island*, the poet persona confronts the 'father artificer,' James Joyce, from whom, through a kind of ventriloquizing, he seeks absolution for his wish to refuse to participate in what is there called 'a cod's game' – 'That subject people stuff is a cod's game,/infantile, like your peasant pilgrimage.' In other words, the 'decent thing,' which is to take a stand in the patriot game ('that subject people stuff'), is rewritten as a losing proposition, as ignoble, a chump's endeavour. By having this delivered as Joyce's decree, Heaney seems to be playing another kind of game, where he not only reinscribes Joyce in the traditional apprehension of him as apolitical or politically bankrupt, but distances himself from the (unpatriotic) sentiment, if not from the dilemma.

3   Boland specifically made this observation about the colonization of women writers in an Irish television (RTE) panel discussion with Mike Murphy on the subject of the omission of women writers from the *Field Day Anthology* (March 4, 1992). I discuss this in 'What's My Line: The Contemporaneity of Eavan Boland,' *Irish University Review* vol. 23 no. 1 (Spring/Summer 1993), p. 101.

4   See, in particular, Boland's two most recent collections, *Outside History: Selected Poems 1980–1990* (New York and London: W. W. Norton & Co., 1990) and *In A Time of Violence* (New York/London: W. W. Norton & Co., 1994), as well as her pamphlet, *A Kind of Scar*. She further addresses the subject in a collection of critical essays forthcoming from Norton in 1995.

5   Lochhead used the expression 'my country of gender' in introductory remarks at a reading for students at the University of Edinburgh in June 1988, which I attended and

taped. In *Mary Queen of Scots Got her Head Chopped Off*, she cross-dresses nation and gender and class, or (ad)dresses one in terms of the other, by having, for example, Elizabeth outfitted as a kind of prom queen (reminding us that this national icon is historically and symbolically always a (pre)sexual object), and each actress play both queen and servant to the other queen. While Boland's early collections such as *In Her Own Image* and *Nightfeed* seem to focus on gender rather than national identity, it could be argued that her second collection, *The War Horse*, significantly brings these together.

6 For discussions of contemporary treatments of the relationship between national and sexual identity in terms of the theoretical use of cross-dressing, see Marge Garber's *Vested Interests: Cross-Dressing and Cultural Anxiety* (New York and London: Routledge, 1992) and in particular her essay, 'The Occidental Tourist: *M. Butterfly* and the Scandal of Transvestism,' in *Nationalisms and Sexualities*, eds., Parker, Andrew, Mary Russo, Doris Sommer and Patricia Yaeger (New York and London: Routledge, 1992), pp. 121–146. Also, see Sandra Gilbert and Susan Gubar *No Man's Land: The Place of the Woman Writer in the Twentieth Century* Vol. 2: Sexchanges (New Haven and London: Yale University Press, 1988); George Mosse, *Nationalism and Sexuality: Respectability and Abnormal Sexuality in Modern Europe* (New York: H. Fertig, 1985).

7 See, for example, Ann Rosalind Jones and Peter Stallybrass, 'Dismantling Irena: The Sexualizing of Ireland in Early Modern England,' in *Nationalisms and Sexualities*, pp. 157–174; Homi K. Bhabha, *Nation and Narration* (London and New York: Routledge, 1990); and George Mosse.

8 Garber briefly takes up the issue of the marginalization and essentialization of women within the transvestite model of liberation from sexual fixity. She concludes that while women remain props rather than 'models', or become, as she puts it, 'risible signs of failed "femininity"' when they cross-dress, men suffer by association from the idea that woman is artifact; if women are constricted, so must be men ('The Occidental Tourist,' pp. 141–2). So, too, the colonized wish to maintain the colonizer as 'other' reveals the same potential anxiety of association that Garber realizes between the sexes.

9 The moment when Fergus first identifies himself as Jimmy is resonant in a number of ways having to do with border crossings. Fergus follows Dil to the Metro after she has cut his hair and in the bar they first interact through Col, identified in the text as 'barman' to begin with, but possessing, like Dil, a gender neutral name. When Dil reports to Col that Fergus is Scottish, Col repeats it with a question – 'Scottish?' – as though in disbelief. Col, who plays the role of a kind of behind-the-scenes, all-knowing duenna, is attuned to performance of all kinds. He participates in the cultural transaction without intervention, acting as a medium, who knows but will not say. And it is equally interesting to note that this cultural transaction takes place after Fergus has had his hair cut, in one mythology a loss of masculinity, in another, the one performed later when Fergus cuts Dil's hair, a loss of femininity.

10 Most historians of the clan system of Scotland agree that the roll call of tartans as it now stands has been largely constructed since the end of the nineteenth century, mostly by the English, and bearing little relation to the clans' historical tartan attire. Because the tartan was identified with the Scots, it was banned by the English government after the Battle of Culloden in 1746. It took almost forty years before the ban was removed and by that time the tartan customs had largely disappeared. See, for example, Robert Bain's *The Clans and Tartans of Scotland* (London and Glasgow: Collins, 1956).

Anne M. McKim

'Makand hir mone': Masculine Constructions of the Feminine Voice in Middle Scots Complaints

Most medieval writers were male and Scottish poets were no exception. Although we can never be certain in the case of anonymous poetry, those Middle Scots poets whose identity is known, including the prominent figures, Henryson, Dunbar, Douglas and Lindsay, were male. All of them, however, impersonated the feminine voice. While most major poets at some point appropriate the feminine voice, especially that of the abandoned woman, there appears to have been something of an upsurge in the use of the feminine voice in late fifteenth and early sixteenth centuries poetry by male authors.[1] Ovid's series of literary ventriloquisations, the *Heroides*, was a primary model for medieval and renaissance poets interested in experimenting with female-voiced laments, especially in epistolary form.[2] In Middle Scots poetry there are a number of framed laments, specifically complaints spoken by wretched female figures, which are embedded in narratives communicated, usually in the first person, by male narrators who are frequently characterised as poets, a device that establishes ironic distance from the speaker, a distance that can vary according to the extent to which distinctions between poet-personae and their creators are blurred. Complaints of this kind often exploit differences between the male narrator's frame and the reported voice of the female in ways which depend integrally on gender, as John Kerrigan has observed:

> It is the pregnant difference between reported voice and the script that conveys it (through a narrator) to the world which underpins contrasts between lamenter figures, and the 'I's who describe them . . . A framing 'I' is hardly ever feminine in medieval poetry. The weight of cultural authority lay so much with men that texts inevitably re-commended what they enclosed with the sanction of 'male' narration.[3]

From a feminist critical point of view, the female speaker whose 'voice' is thus mediated is not a textual subject but an object invented by a male author engaged in literary cross-dressing often in order to address other men. As a recent collection of essays on the depiction of women in medieval and renaissance male-authored texts demonstrates, male writings in these periods 'referred to, responded to, manipulated, and projected desire upon other men and other men's writings'.[4] The Middle Scots poets whose complaints are examined in the present essay are acutely aware of working in a male poetic tradition, or what has been described as a 'homotextual' tradition, when they appropriate the feminine voice.[5]

MAID TO REPORT THE LAMENTATION . . .

The best known, certainly the most accomplished, example of female-voiced complaint in Middle Scots poetry is that of Cresseid, in Robert Henryson's late fifteenth-century *Testament of Cresseid*.[6] The reporting frame is established in the opening lines with the elderly narrator sitting down to write a 'tragedie', while in the final stanza of the poem the poet-narrator concludes with a reference to the making of 'this ballat schort' (410).[7] The literary nature of his undertaking is further underscored by his allusions early in the poem to reading Chaucer's *Troilus and Criseyde* (40–60) but more illuminating still are his comments on the 'vther quair' which represent this almost certainly fictitious source of the *Testament* as a male-authored female-voiced complaint: 'Be sum poeit, throw his inventioun,/Maid to report the lamentatioun'[8] as well as the 'wofull end' (67–9) of Cresseid. Such a summary might very well serve as a paradigm for the genre, one which highlights gender stereotypes: the lamenter is a female whose words are invented, imagined, by a male poet, with the weight of cultural authority behind him, who purports to be a mere reporter. No sooner has the narrator of the *Testament* defined the 'vther quair' as an unidentified male poet's imaginative record of Cresseid's 'lamentatioun', or complaint, and her tragic death, than a seamless shift from the frame to the story of Cresseid's 'fatall destenie' (62) allows the spurious text and the narrator's account to merge and become one (70–71). The actual existence, or rather non-existence, of the 'vther quair' is immaterial: the impression cultivated is of a male textual tradition, in which homage is duly paid to literary predecessors, including 'worthie Chaucer glorious' (41), while a spirit of friendly rivalry produces the banter of:

> 'Quha wait gif all that Chauceir wrait was trew?
> Nor I wait nocht gif this narratioun
> Be authoreist, or fenyeit of the new.
>
> (64–6)

Even while he appears to question he affirms the importance of *auctoritas*.

Cresseid's Complaint (407–69) is a formal rhetorical piece, written in the nine-line stanza conventionally employed for complaint, (which distinguishes it from the rest of the poem which is in the seven-line rhyme royal stanza), and is introduced, as such complaints frequently are, by a phrase that identifies the genre as well as the tone:

> And on this wyse, weiping, scho maid hir mone
> (406)

while a return to the narrator's perspective is signalled with:

> Thus chydand with hir drerie destenye,
> Weiping scho woik the nicht fra end to end;
> Bot all in vane; hir dule, hir cairfull cry,
> Micht not remeid, not yit hir murning mend
> (470–73)

The frame distances the reader from the speaker, so that her 'mone' is clearly mediated by what Cerquiglini has called the 'master of the game,' the poet whose representation of the discourse of others is in fact a 'manipulation'.[9]

While complaints on the theme of fortune by both male and female speakers are common enough in medieval literature and, like others, Cresseid's Complaint is Boethian in its preoccupation with reversals of Fortune,[10] it contains a number of features which have been identified as distinguishing lyrics written from a female perspective or in a female persona: in particular a sense of helplessness, pessimism, and resignation before the power of Fortune.[11] The first stanza alone conveys all three, before climaxing in Cresseid's rather desperate wish for death:

> 'O sop of sorrow, sonkin into cair,
> O catiue Cresseid, now and euer mair
> Gane is thy ioy and all thy mirth in eird;
> Of all blyithnes now art thou blaiknit bair;
> Thair is na salue may saif or sound thy sair!
> Fell is thy fortoun, wickit is thy weird,
> Thy blys is baneist, and thy baill on breird!
> Vnder the eirth, God gif I grauin wer,
> Quhair nane of Grece nor yit of Troy micht heird!
> (407–15)

That the gender of the speaker is an issue can be readily demonstrated when Cresseid's Complaint is compared to the complaint uttered by another of Henryson's tragic characters, Orpheus in *Orpheus and Eurydice*. After the abduction of his beloved Eurydice, Orpheus laments his terrible loss in terms which superficially resemble Cresseid's Complaint. But whereas Cresseid has been deprived of her 'hie estait' ((437) and the symbols of that status (416–33) Orpheus decides to abdicate his royal position, to divest himself of various worldly trappings (157–160). The *ubi sunt* motif in the *Testament* conveys her regret for what she has irrevocably lost ('all is areir'), whereas Orpheus is portrayed as having the power of choice, as the repeated use of the future tense indicates:

> My rob ryall and all my riche array
> Changit *sall* be in rude russat of gray;
> My diademe in till ane hat of hair;
> My bed *sall* be with beaver, broke, and bair, . . .
> (157–160, my italics)

Orpheus can contemplate a future because he retains some optimism: in other words, he believes his situation can improve, that a change for the better can be effected with the help of his gods, Phoebus and Jupiter:

> on thee I call
> To mend my murnyng and my drery mone
> (175–6)

These were the very gods whose beneficent influence did not operate in Cresseid's case, so she was led to the dismal conclusion: 'Thair is na salue may saif or sound thy sair!' (411). The utterances of Cresseid in the *Testament* – which include an angry address to Venus and Cupid (126–40), a confession (542–74) and testament (577–91) as well as her formal complaint – make her rhetorically dominant, in a poem in which she is strikingly powerless, the situation of numerous female speakers of medieval laments and songs.[12]

SCHE SPAK . . . I HERD

The *Testament of Cresseid* is an exceptional poem, and quite unlike other extant Middle Scots complaint literature in, for instance, the number of lines allocated to Cresseid's 'speech', her character's previous existence, as it were, in other texts, notably Chaucer's *Troilus*, and the intertextual aspect of her speaking as a consequence.[13] Elsewhere in Middle Scots poetry, reported discourse is often represented, (as in many English and continental analogues), as overheard by the narrator figure. In the highly stylised introduction of the anonymous fifteenth-century work, 'The Quare of Jelusy',[14] for example, the narrator describes how while walking and brooding on some undisclosed personal sorrow in a beautiful garden one fine May morning he[15] overhears the complaint of a newly married lady whose suffering is caused by her husband's apparently groundless jealousy, allying her with the figure of the unhappy wife of the French *chanson de mal mariée*. The lady's complaint (59–92), which takes the form of an impassioned appeal to two female deities, first Hymen, incorrectly identified as 'goddesse' of marriage, and then Diana, 'goddesse of fredome and of ese' (77), to whom she repeatedly proclaims her innocence of any offence, inspires the poet-narrator to write a lengthy treatise, or 'trety in the reprefe of Ielousye':

> for this ladies sak,
> Sa mekle occupacioun schall I tak
> Furthwith for to syttyn doun and writt
> Of Ielouse folk sum thing into dispitt.
> (153–156)

Although the narrator had initially refused to divulge the 'suffrance and the peyne' constraining his own heart:

> The quhich as now me nedith not report
> (27)

> And to no wicht I will compleyne nor mene
> (30)

after hearing the lady's complaint he is moved to voice his own complaint, on behalf of women, one which emulates the tone of female-voiced lament and employs the most characteristic marker, or signature, of such feminine discourse, 'alas':

> 'Allace, the wo! quho can it specify
> That wommen suffren ay withoutyn quhy.
> (227–8)
> Quho schall me help, allace, for to endite,
> For to bewaill, to compleyne, and to write
> This vice, that now so large is and commoun?
> (245–7)

Among other things, the *Quare of Jelusy* is a poem *about* speaking for women, and appropriating the female voice is one means of doing so. At the same time, the poet-narrator's frequent references to his writing, including expressions of anxiety about his lack of poetic skills (159–62; 178; 185–90; 245–47; 308–16; 582–89), keep his role and presence to the fore of a poem whose very title draws attention to its literariness.

In the *Quare*, almost as soon as he glimpses the lady in the beautiful garden, the narrator admits: 'preuely I hid me of entent / Among the levis to here quhat sche ment' (45–6). That he is apparently prompted to this behaviour by supposing she might be Diana suggests that he himself resembles Actaeon whose voyeurism was summarily punished when he was hunted and torn to pieces by his own hounds.[16] Recent theories of looking connect the male gaze with gender and power: when woman is turned into 'an object – and most particularly an object of vision: a sight' not only desire but control is asserted since the 'male gaze signifies the power of men over women, the power to define women as objects or commodities'.[17] The male narrator in framed plaints watches and listens, ostensibly to report what he sees and hears. Indeed, female-voiced complaints in Middle Scots poetry, owing something to the French *chanson d'aventure*, are often depicted as overheard monologues, and these overheard monologues are delivered as if no other human is present.[18] In the *Quare of Jelusy*, the female lamenter figure believes herself to be alone: she speaks so quietly that the narrator has some difficulty in hearing her (53–4), she curses Jealousy 'preualy' (55) and, believing herself to be alone (85), she maintains that her innocence needs no publication as 'thilk hid thing' (86) is already known to her gods.

The best and most outrageous example of eavesdropping in Middle Scots poetry is, of course, in William Dunbar's *Tretis of the Tua Mariit Wemen and the Wedo* (c. 1508). In this 'female-centred poem'[19] the narrator is characterised as going to some lengths to conceal his presence from the three women (the two wives and widow of the title) he comes across around midnight one midsummer's eve. He tells how he 'drewe in derne to the dyke eftir mirthis' (9) and on hearing a human voice quickly hides in a hawthorn hedge, his undignified alacrity injecting humour into the scene:

> With that in haist to the hege so hard I inthrang
> That I was heildit with hawthorne and with heynd leveis
> (13–14)[20]

Thus concealed, the narrator spies and eavesdrops on the women.

As a literary device eavesdropping usefully allows the narrator to present himself as merely the instrument of revelation, as one who reports what he happened to overhear. The link between clandestine watching and listening and writing is made explicit in the *Tua Mariit Wemen* when the women leave in the morning,

And I all prevely past to a plesand arber,
And with my pen did *report* thair pastance most mery.
(525–26, my emphasis)

What is more, readers are implicated in the eavesdropping when at the end of the poem the narrator addresses them as 'Ye auditoris'. The directness of the address also reminds us of the poem's first and possibly physically present audience at the Scottish court of James IV, and that this irreverent and satirical poem was presented as an entertainment to, one supposes, appreciative listeners. The extent to which Dunbar parodies traditional genres like the *chanson d'aventure*, the *chanson de mal mariée* and the *demande d'amour* has been discussed elsewhere.[21] The confessional mode in which the three women speak promotes the impression that secrets are disclosed but, as a recent reading highlights, the poem ultimately reveals more about the nature of male fantasy about women's sexuality than about the nature of women.[22] The supreme irony has to be that a poem which purports to reveal what women say about men in men's absence actually exposes what men have said about women in their absence as subjects in male-authored texts.

I DID MY DELYGENCE AND CURE / TO LERNE HIR LANGUAGE ARTIFICIALL

While it was the 'sugarat sound' of a bird's song that first drew the narrator to the hawthorn hedge in Dunbar's poem, in Sir David Lyndsay's *Testament and Complaynt of Our Soverane Lordis Papyngo* (1530)[23] it is actually a bird that utters the complaint covertly overheard and reported by the narrator. A royal female parrot is characterised as a plaintful figure moved, after a fatal fall from a treetop, to contemplate the vicissitudes of fortune, in language evocatively reminiscent of Cresseid's Complaint.[24] Moreover, Lyndsay's chosen title inevitably recalls that by which Henryson's poem was known from at least the early sixteenth century.

The Testament of the Papyngo is a work that ostentatiously parades its literariness in a number of ways. In the prologue to his 'pieteous taill' (75), the poet-narrator pays homage to his literary ancestors in one of the most elaborate reworkings of the conventional modesty *topos* in Middle Scots poetry. Having listed the many Scottish poets, including Henryson and Dunbar, as well as paying the customary homage to the English triumvirate, Chaucer, Gower and Lydgate, who have already denuded the garden of eloquence, Lyndsay confesses 'I watt nocht quhat to wryte' (56), so he proposes to 'declare . . . The complaynt of ane woundit Papyngo' (62–3). What follows is a small rhetorical miscellany comprising her complaint, two epistles, to the king and his courtiers respectively, as well as a fable, and finally an epilogue which brings the whole work to a conclusion and restores the frame:

Now have ye hard this lytill tragedie,
   The sore complent, the testament, and myschance
   Of this pure bird,

(1170–72)

with the focus returning to the poet as writer of this 'quair' (1175).

Just as awareness of poetic tradition informs Lyndsay's prologue, so familiarity with the conventions of literary complaint, whereby this private utterance is overheard by the male narrator so he in turn can make it public, is evident in the poem.[25] So although the poet-narrator relates how he was given charge of the king's parrot and how one morning, as was his custom, he went into his garden with the bird on his hand, the conventions of the *chanson d'aventure* and complaint are consciously evoked.[26]

A description of an encounter does not ensue since the narrator is accompanied, as he walks around the garden, by the bird who will utter the complaint. Yet when the fatally injured bird 'gan to mak hir mone' (173) she immediately becomes identified with other female lamenter figures, even to the point of swooning as a preliminary to her complaint (190–91), and the narrator, too, identifies himself with the role of male eavesdropper who, moved to tears, hides himself under the ubiquitous hawthorn tree to listen secretly:

> To heir that birdis lamentatioun,
> I did aproche, onder ane hauthorne grene,
> *Quhare I mycht heir and se, and be unsene*;
> (187–9, my italics)

By deliberately and humorously employing the conventions of framed complaint, Lyndsay effectively highlights the constructed and gendered nature of the assigned roles. He goes further: he draws attention to the ventriloquistic nature of the genre. The central figure in the poem is the parrot, traditionally renowned for its mimicry, 'of hir Inclynatioun naturall Scho countrafaitit' (*Testament of the Papyngo*, 89–90). One of the narrator's tasks as keeper of the king's parrot is to teach her to speak 'language artificiall' (87) in order that she may entertain the royal court with her mimicry, as well as by her display of other tricks (88). He teaches her to imitate the human voice, but of course the bird's repertoire is limited to what she has been taught to say, that is, only to what he desires her to say. In the case of the two epistles which follow the parrot's complaint, it is obvious that the bird serves as a mouthpiece, voicing the poet's advice first to the king and then to the court. In this respect the parrot functions like a ventriloquist's puppet which only appears to utter words that are in fact projected by a controlling figure. Her position on the narrator's hand ('I bure hir on my hande' (100)) even suggests the ventriloquist's puppet.

As a poet, Lyndsay imitates earlier poets who had impersonated female voices in complaints and succeeds in demonstrating that such literary mimicry is essentially an aptitude for imitating the characteristic voice of the Other, as defined and bequeathed by male poets.[27] Moreover, if, as Roland Barthes has claimed, 'the 'I' which appears in the text is already itself a plurality of other texts',[28] in the case of reported discourse, which much of *The Testament of the Papyngo* purports to be, both the narratorial 'I' and the lamenting 'I' can be described as pluralities, evoking other voices and other texts.[29]

Lyndsay's female complainer is a parrot, not a woman, so it comes as no surprise that the affinity with fable is developed more fully in the last – and longest – part of the poem, 'The Commonyng betuix the Papingo and her Holye Executouris', a dialogue between the parrot and a magpie, a raven and a kite, which constitutes a trenchant satire on ecclesiastical vices. Fables, too, relying on personification as they do, are ventriloquisations in which 'brutall beistis spak and vnderstude', in Henryson's view, for the purpose of exemplifying 'How many men in operatioun/ Are like to beistis in conditioun.'[30] In exposing human behaviour, especially human pretensions, through the use of animal protagonists, Henryson's fables inevitably reveal human stereotypes, as well as some of the socially constructed roles. In the 'Cock and the Fox', for instance, the cock's fate is a consequence of masculine posturing and pride. The fox dupes him by tempting him into a father-son rivalry by questioning the eligibility of the 'son and heir' (470). The hens, on the other hand, are depicted as fickle and sexually voracious females, like Dunbar's *wedo* and two wives, whose utterly insincere lament is a wonderful parody of the traditional female lament.

But the fable in which Henryson is most experimental with the female-voiced complaint is the 'Lion and the Mouse'. The fable is distinguished from the other *Morall Fabillis* by a prologue in the form of a dream allegory. Like the narrators of the *Quare* and the *Testament of the Papyngo*, the poet-narrator is walking in a beautiful landscape, the conventional *locus amoenus*, but instead of an encounter with a plaintful female figure, the narrator, resting in the shade of a hawthorn tree, dreams he meets his *auctor*, Aesop. There is no need for surreptitious conduct here: Aesop comes through the thicket (1347) and the narrator becomes a keen listener when his 'maister venerabill' (1384) is persuaded to relate 'ane morall fabill' (1401). What is more, Aesop several times addresses the narrator as 'sone' and he in turn responds by calling the fabulist 'father' as well as 'maister', figuring a hereditary succession or relationship between classical *auctor* and vernacular *makar*,[31] but also suggesting the patriarchal hegemony in which male authors are the custodians of culture and morality. Henryson had introduced his fable collection as 'ane maner of translatioun' (32) of Aesop which allowed the ancient fabulist to speak through him, but in assigning the fable of 'The Lion and Mouse' to Aesop he specifically represents this fable as reported discourse, one that can be designated ventriloquistic.[32]

The fable is an allegory about relations of power, as the *moralitas* makes clear (lines 1595–1600), and it is noteworthy that Henryson chooses in the narrative to depict such relations in gendered terms: the lion is male and powerful, 'lord and king/Off beistis all' (lines 1430–31), 'mychtie' (1436) and 'strang' (1483, 1494), while the mouse is female, inferior (1427, 1493) and defenceless (1487). On the two occasions in the fable that the mouse is referred to as a male – first as 'the maister mous' (1418) who leads the other mice in their impudent 'trace' (1413) across the sleeping lion, and later when she calls on them to free the captured lion from ropes, and they reply 'Ye, gude brother' (1558) – her identification as a leader seems to warrant the masculine designation for this role. It would be a mistake, I believe, to dismiss these apparent inconsistencies as slips on Henryson's part, especially as the same 'error' does not occur in the presentation of his male animals, none of whom, including the lion, is ever referred to as female. (One could take this matter of gendered roles further by asking why it is impossible to imagine the tod, for example, as female.)

Indeed much of the comedy in the *Lion and Mouse* is generated by such shrewd observation of the conventionalised nature of male-female roles. Henryson exploits traditional gender roles which identify the (female) mouse as small and weak and helpless and the (male) lion as dominant and strong and powerful. In her appeal to the lion for royal mercy, his masculinity is flattered by her allusion to one of the most traditional measures of manliness, prowess in battle (1475–81), a parallel which is then beautifully debunked by her conclusion:

> Ane thowsand myis to kill and eik deuoir
> Is lytill manheid to ane strang lyoun
> (1482–3)

It is significant then that the complaint Henryson assigns to the captured lion later in the poem resembles Cresseid's Complaint in a number of respects, the most obvious of which are noted by Fox:

The lion's formal and traditional lament is very similar to the lament of Cresseid in the *Testament*. Line 1530 resembles the line which introduces Cresseid's lament, 'And on this wyse, weiping, scho maid hir mone' (406); there is the same initial self-apostrophe ('O sop of sorrow ... O catiue Cresseid'); the same rhetorical use of the *ubi sunt* theme (*Fables* 1532; *Testament* 416, 425); the same antithesis between former glory and present misery (*Fables* 1532–7, *Testament* 434–7, etc.); and the same expression of hopelessness (*Fables* 1537–9, *Testament* 411, 455).[33]

Although Fox goes on to refer the reader to Orpheus's lament in *Orpheus and Eurydice* (133ff) as well, the same kind of parallels cannot, in fact, be drawn, for although framed in much the same way as Henryson's other complaints ('thusgait he maid his mone', 133 and 'Quhen endit was the sangis lamentable', 184) the tenor of this complaint is quite different. What is more, although he is distraught with 'dule and wo', Orpheus does not regard himself as fortune's victim, nor does he express, as I mentioned earlier, the sense of helplessness, hopelessness or resignation found in the complaints of Cresseid and the lion, recognised aspects of female-voiced laments. The powerlessness of the fettered lion is identified as a feminised state: he begins by expressing his changed condition as a form of emasculation:

> O *lamit* lyoun, liggand heir sa law,
> Quhair is the mycht off thy magnyfycence,
> (1531–32, my italics)

and the ignominy of his plight lies in his sense of utter subjection, for his is now the vulnerability of the abandoned (literally *reduced to subjection, subdued*)[34] female, and his plaint even includes that recurrent marker of feminine discourse, 'alas':

> But hoip or help, but succour or defence,
> In bandis strang heir man I ly, allace,
> Till I be slane; I se nane vther grace.
> (1535–37)

For the lion, reversal of fortune is analogous not only to a reversal of situations (the captured mouse's plight becomes the lion's), but also to a reversal of roles. The reversal becomes complete when the characteristically feminine lament assigned to the male lion is overheard by the female mouse (1530–1544).

Henryson's interest in experimenting with an inherited genre like the complaint is evident in the *Testament* too. He found in Chaucer's Troilus a feminised hero:

> The story in which he is set casts him in a feminine role in that it assimilates him to the women of Ovid's *Heroides* – abandoned and betrayed by his lover, immobilised, frustrated of action and

movement, finding relief only in memory, lamentation and fruitless letter-writing.[35]

In the *Testament*, Troilus's plight as an abandoned lover associates him with female lamenter figures. On hearing of Cresseid's 'greit infirmitie,/Hir legacie and lamentatioun' (596–7), he swoons and expresses the briefest of laments:

> 'I can no moir;
> Scho was vntrew and wo is me thairfoir.'
> (601–2)

There is no mistaking the helplessness, hopelessness and resignation more usual in female-voiced complaints.

For all that, in Henryson's poem Troilus's final affinity is with the male narrator. According to 'sum' says the narrator, Troilus built a tomb for Cresseid on which he engraved 'hir name and superscriptioun' (604). He encloses her body as the poet has her voice in a construction of his making:

> Sum said he maid ane tomb of merbeill gray,
> And wrait hir name and superscriptioun,
> And laid it on hir graue quhair that scho lay,
> In goldin letteris, conteining this ressoun:
> 'Lo, fair ladyis, Cresseid of Troy the toun,
> Sumtyme countit the flour of womanheid,
> Vnder this stane, lait liper, lyis deid.'
> (603–9)

This tomb bears his text, his 'ressoun', which echoes the words earlier ascribed to Cresseid in her Complaint:

> O ladyis fair of Troy and Grece, attend
> (452)

And her admonition to these same ladies:

> Nocht is your fairness bot ane faiding flour
> (461)

Troilus's writing, his 'goldin letteris', re-present and interpret Cresseid by recycling the words the narrator had already used to represent her voice, her speaking. Although there is an attempt by the narrator at distance ('sum said'), his concluding stanza more or less repeats and so seems to endorse Troilus's summary:

Now, worthie women

evoking the 'lo, fair ladyis', while the final line:

Sen scho is deid I speik of hir no moir

echoes Troilus's 'I can no moir'. The suggestive equivalency of text and tomb, the ultimate confined space, has powerful implications.

ECCO . . . I THE BESEKE THOU HELPETH ME TO FLYTE

'For a male author to write women' in the Middle Ages and Renaissance, observe Fisher and Halley, 'was to refer not to women, but to men – to desire not relationship with women, but relationship to the traditions of male textual activity'.[36] The Middle Scots examples of male-authored female-voiced complaints briefly considered in this essay offer striking substantiation of this view. Their authors are expressly aware of working in a poetic tradition and to varying degrees of engaging preceding and fellow poets as rivals. The use of the feminine voice for this interchange provides these poets with a challenging opportunity to exercise their *inuentioun*, to impersonate not only the feminine voice but through that impersonation to evoke, often ironically, other voices and other texts. ❦

University of Waikato

1   Lawrence Lipking, *Abandoned Women and Poetic Tradition* (Chicago, 1988) p. 127 and John Kerrigan (ed) *Motives of Woe: Shakespeare and 'Female Complaint', A Critical Anthology* (Oxford, 1991), p. 1.
2   A late medieval Scottish example of such an epistolary lament is 'The Laste Epistle of Creseyd to Troyalus' (c. 1590) attributed, but as a poem of doubtful authenticity, to William Fowler in *The Works of William Fowler* ed. Henry Meikle, 3 vols. STS, 6, 7, 13 (1914–40), vol. I, pp. 379–87.
3   John Kerrigan, *Motives of Woe*, pp. 11–12.
4   Sheila Fisher and Janet Halley (eds) *Seeking the Woman in Late Medieval and Renaissance Writings: Essays in Feminist Contextual Criticism* (Knoxville, 1989), p. 4.
5   Ibid.
6   *The Poems of Robert Henryson* ed. Denton Fox (Oxford, 1981). All references to Henryson are to this edition. I have normalized yogh to *y* or *gh*. The earliest surviving printed editions of *The Testament* are those by William Thynne (London, 1532) and Henry Charteris (Edinburgh 1593). Both printers identify the complaint by a separate rubric.
7   This is something of a vexed critical question because the tone differs from that of the narrator earlier in the poem. Matthew Pittock has recently attempted to explain the inconsistencies by an ingenious theory of complex narration in which he identifies a number

of narratorial masks worn by Henryson in the *Testament*. 'The Complexity of Henryson's *The Testament of Cresseid*', *Essays in Criticism* XI, no. 3 (July 1990), 198–221.

8 *Lamentatioun*, like *mone*, is a common synonym for *compleynt* in the works under consideration.

9 Bernard Cerquiglini, 'The Syntax of Discursive Authority: The Example of Feminine Discourse', *Yale French Studies* 70 (1986), p. 184.

10 For parallels between Cresseid's Complaint and that of Boethius against Fortune (*De Consolatione Philosophiae* I, *metrum* 4) see McKim, 'Henryson's "Memoriall of Fair Cresseid"' in *Of Lion and Of Unicorn: Essays on Anglo-Scottish Literary Relations in Honour of Professor John MacQueen* ed. R. D. S. Jack and K. McGinley (Edinburgh, 1993), pp. 8–9.

11 Elizabeth Hanson-Smith, 'A Woman's View of Courtly Love: The Findern Anthology', *Journal of Women's Studies in Literature* 1, no. 3 (1979), 179–94. Sarah McNamer, 'Female Author, Provincial Setting: The Re-versing of Courtly Love in the Findern Manuscript', *Viator* 22 (1991), 279–310.

12 See Maureen Fries, 'The "other" voice: woman's song, its satire, and its transcendence in late medieval British literature' in *Vox Feminae: Studies in Medieval Women's Songs* ed. John F. Plummer (Kalamazoo, 1981), p. 169.

13 I have explored some of the implications of this intertextuality in 'Henryson's "Memoriall of Fair Cresseid"' and 'Tracing the Ring: Henryson, Fowler, and Chaucer's *Troilus*', *Notes & Queries* (Dec. 1993), pp. 449–51.

14 The title is provided by the rubric in the only known source for this poem, MS. Bodley Arch. Seld. B. 24, which also contains the *Kingis Quair*. I have quoted from the edition prepared by J. Norton-Smith and I. Pravda, *The Quare of Jelusy* (Heidelberg, 1976).

15 The narrator uses the masculine pronoun to refer to himself at line 158.

16 A number of examples where the concealed poet is characterized as another Actaeon are discussed by A. C. Spearing, *The medieval poet as voyeur: looking & listening in medieval love-narratives* (Cambridge, 1993), pp. 35–39.

17 Spearing, who draws on John Berger's *Ways of Seeing* in his examination of the role of looking in medieval love-narratives, p. 23.

18 Although this is not the case with Cresseid's Complaint, she chooses to hide herself in a dark corner of the spittal house, 'allone' (405). Also, while the *Testament*'s elderly narrator warming himself by the fire on a winter-like night could hardly be more different from the perambulating narrator of the *Quare* and other framed amatory plaints, and his relationship with her is conditioned by her role as a fictional character he has read about, at a number of points what Cresseid 'says' is overheard.

19 Maureen Fries, 168.

20 *The Poems of William Dunbar* ed. J. Small, STS 2, 4, 16 (1890). All quotations from Dunbar are from this edition.

21 Denton Fox, 'Scottish Chaucerians', *Chaucer and Chaucerians: Critical Studies in Middle English Literature*, ed. D. S. Brewer (London & Edinburgh, 1966), pp. 164ff.

22 Spearing, 266. John Plummer has noted that many medieval lyrics written from a female perspective are confessions embodying male fantasies about female sexuality. 'The Woman's Song in Middle English and its European Backgrounds' in *Vox Feminae*, p. 139.

23 *The Works of Sir David Lindsay* ed. Douglas Hamer, Scottish Text Society, Third series, Nos. 1, 2, 4, 8 (Edinburgh, 1931–6). All quotations are from this edition.

24 E.g. *Testament of the Papyngo* 171, 173, 204, 217–19, 220 and *Testament of Cresseid* 350, 406, 550 & 602, 141.

25 Spearing discusses the poet-narrator's role in making the private public in Chapter 1 of *The medieval poet as voyeur*.

26 The beautiful garden and the birdsong in particular. There are verbal echoes of Chaucer's *Parliament of Fowls*, but there are also debts to the poetry of Dunbar and Douglas. Janet H. Williams has traced verbal echoes of Dunbar in another of his works, 'The Complaynt of Schir Dauid Lindesay' in '"Althocht I beir nocht lyke ane baird": David Lyndsay's "Complaynt"', *Scottish Literary Journal* vol. 9, No. 2 (Dec. 1982), 5–20 (6–9).

27 My own text here appropriates and modifies the *OED* definition of mimicry.

28 Barthes, *S/Z*, 10 quoted by H. Marshall Leicester, *The Disenchanted Self: Representing the Subject in the Canterbury Tales* (Berkeley, 1990), 133.

29 'An intertextual allusion opens a text to other voices and echoes of other texts, just as ventriloquism multiplies authorial voices', Harvey, *Ventriloquized Voices*, p. 10.

30 Henryson, *Prologue* to the *Morall Fabillis*, 44, 48–49.

31 Machan, 'Robert Henryson and Father Aesop: Authority in the *Morall Fables*', *Studies in the Age of Chaucer* vol. 12 (1990), 206.

32 Machan comments: 'In the first six fables Aesop is imaged to stand figuratively behind Henryson and speak through him, here [Lion and Mouse] Henryson stands behind the ancient and, by claiming to offer direct quotation of him, situates the origin of the author's dialogue and fable in himself' (p. 209).

33 *Commentary* 1530–44, p. 271.

34 *DOST* s.v. *Abandoun* and Lipking, *Abandoned Women and Poetic Tradition*, p. xvii.

35 Jill Mann, *Geoffrey Chaucer* (Cambridge, 1991), p. 168.

36 *Seeking the Woman in Late Medieval and Renaissance Writings*, p. 4.

AILEEN CHRISTIANSON

Rewriting Herself: Jane Welsh Carlyle's Letters

I have so much to tell and so little time to tell it in that I don't know where to begin. (27 Feb. 1849, Huxley 321)

This is how Jane Welsh Carlyle starts one of her letters to her cousin Jeannie in 1849 and this is also how I feel at writing a short paper on Jane's letterwriting practices after editing her letters for 25 years. As the wife of Thomas Carlyle, that great Scottish Victorian monolith, and because of her skill as a letter-writer, Jane is assumed by many to be a 'missing' woman writer, oppressed or peripheralised by her role as the wife of a 'great writer'. The truth of her situation is less stereotyped and more interesting. This article looks at the way in which she practised the very specific literary skill of letter writing.

We see letterwriting now as a legitimate literary genre, part of life-writing, which demands particular artistic choices and skills. Jane used these skills to dramatise and orchestrate her life materials, providing at times a subversive subtext to Thomas's own view of himself. Jane had a 'private writing career' (to use Elizabeth Hardwick's phrase in *Seduction and Betrayal*, 174) which paralleled Thomas's public writing career, amateur to his professional. What we have to do is see her writing as evidence of a chosen response to her life rather than hints of lost, unwritten novels. This response of Jane's allowed an ongoing interaction, an opportunity to mould that life into entertainment for others, and provided a safety valve or outlet (entirely within her control) through which she could obliquely or directly express her feelings. Her surviving letters indicate a preference for indirection rather than direct complaint, presented as a gallant wit in the face of adversity. She rarely articulated any extensive analysis of her own character but by foregrounding her life with Thomas, whether described with zest, pathos, self-depreciation, humour or irritation, she provided a structure of material for analysis visible to any careful reader. To paraphrase Mary Poovey, Jane made statements about herself by directing attention to people around her, making herself known by drawing attention to the relationship of which she was part. (Poovey 45)

The main recipients of Jane's letters, after her mother's death in 1842, were her cousins Jeannie and Helen Welsh, and the writer Geraldine Jewsbury. They were primed to interpret her sympathetically, from a Jane-inspired point of view. Most of her letters to Jewsbury were destroyed at her request so the largest surviving series of her letters are those to her cousins. In using them for interpretational analysis, we have to allow for the possible self-censorship imposed by the probability that her uncle, her mother's brother, would also see them.

Jeannie and Helen were in some way interchangeable for Jane; when one was away from home, or when Jeannie got married, the other became the recipient; that is to say they were the excuse for Jane creating the letters, rather than being the particularly chosen, individuated recipient.

To illustrate this, here are two opening paragraphs, the first to Helen, and the second to Jeannie, both discussing the function of letter writing:

> If you were a Socinian, duly inspired by the precept 'Let your care be the welfare of others' you would not give way to those long fits of silence; for a letter from you always promotes my welfare, considerably, for the time being. You write very nice letters and you are a very nice cousin, and I have no fault to find with you but that you are not sufficiently sensible of your own importance to me.
>
> For *me*; I am incorrigible as to the 'welfare of others' – at least in the matter of letter writing the idea of *giving pleasure* cannot prevail with me to write and I write always from one of two motives, from a *need* to *receive* a letter, only to be extracted by *giving* one, or from gratitude for what is vouchsafed me 'on the voluntary principle'. The latter motive sets my pen agoing just now – and an exceedingly bad pen it is! – Jeannie having been a better correspondent lately has kept me up with the current of your affairs, and I trusted *her* to keep you up with the current of mine. (23 Oct. 1848, MS NLS 1893.146)

The references to Socinians, the 'welfare of others,' the 'voluntary principle', in this letter are changed in the second example to Jeannie into a reference to Unitarians:

> Upon my honour, dearest Babbie, I am afraid you are growing into a – Unitarian – You heap coals of fire on my head with such an air of unconscious amiability! – not that unconsciousness of all things is a distinctive feature of unitarianism but the *amiability*! – it is *more* than Christian this writing away – all the same as if your letters got duly

answered – well! you do quite right – it is the only way of touching me in certain periods of devil-possessedness – in which periods by the way, the most striking symptom is a horror at letter-writing, similar to the horror mad-dogs conceive at water – (3 Apr. 1849, Huxley 328)

We can see in both extracts her presentation of herself as rather interesting and unconventional in contrast to the duller and worthier Socinians and Unitarians. She expresses very clearly her emotional need for receiving letters, as well as a recognition of being part of a process.

In May 1849, she briefly touches on her silence and Jeannie's forbearance:

And it is rational of *you* as well as patient and good, to believe that my silence has not been this time more than any other time the natural expression of my feeling towards you. – the more I have to say to you always, the less I like to write – the things I have to say being for most part Lamentations of Jeremiah, for which transient human breath is only too good. To *write* lamentations has always you know been contrary to my ideas – (Huxley 325–26)

Jeannie was the cousin who had stayed with Jane in London in 1842 after Jane's mother's death. Jane had also gone to stay in Liverpool in 1846 when she left Thomas in anger over his foolish devotion to Lady Harriet Baring. Both areas of pain had clearly been open to Jeannie in conversation, though Jane rarely alludes to it so directly in her letters – as she says: 'The more I have to say to you always, the less I like to write'.

Elsewhere she hints at the way letter-writing provided a means of controlling the pain of her life by converting it into amusing tales. A letter of 1843 to Amalie Bölte, a German feminist who earned her living as a governess, begins with a denunciation of an apparent complaint that she owed a letter:

Are you become so inoculated with the commercial spirit of this England that you will no longer write to me but on the debtor-and-creditor-principle? Am I no longer to have any *privileges* – moi? No longer to receive two or three or even four letters for one, in consideration of my worries and my indolence? So *you* at least seem to have resolved! – but thank heaven there are still generous spirits among my correspondents who despise such balancing of accounts! who rain down letters on me 'thick as autumnal leaves' without asking even whether I read them! – And you think no shame of yourself, cold blooded calculating little German that you are? Well then, open your ledger and set down now in black and white – 'Mademoiselle Bölte debtor to Mrs Carlyle – in one letter – to be paid immediately – *no credit given.*' (23 Dec. 1843 *CL* 17:208)

This is an earlier more dramatic version of her recognition of a continuing need to be part of a letter-writing process and exchange.

Before she turns to vivid descriptions and complaints about life in winter with a Thomas struggling to write *Cromwell*, Jane carries on with a statement about her emotional control – unusually frank in its mannered way:

What *are* you doing, and thinking, and wishing, and hoping – for in Devonshire I suppose people can still *hope* – even in December – *here* the thing is impossible – . . . And many things besides *speranza* have to be thrown over board as well. To keep one's soul and body together seems to be quite as much as one is *up to* under the circumstances. *I attempt* nothing more – as there is nothing which I so much detest as FAILURE where I have *willed*, so I take precious care never to *will* anything as to which I have a presentiment of *failing* – My husband is more imprudent, he goes on still *willing* to write this *Life of Cromwell* under the most desperate apprehensions that it will 'never come to anything.' (*CL* 17.209)

This is followed by a vigorous description of Thomas's misery over *Cromwell*, 'the grim concentrated self-complacency' with which he burnt 'all his labour since he returned from Scotland.' She continues:

to tell you a secret, I begin to be seriously afraid that his *Life of Cromwell* is going to have the same strange fate as the child of a certain french-marchioness that I once read of – which never could *get itself born*, tho' carried about in her for *twenty years* till she died! – a wit is said to have once asked this poor woman if 'Madame was not thinking of swallowing a tutor for her son?' So one might ask Carlyle if he is not thinking of swallowing a publisher for his book. – only that he is too miserable poor fellow without the addition of being laughed at. (*CL* 17: 210)

This outrageous story allows her specifically to laugh at him behind his back and she ends this passage with an articulation of the function of her story telling:

Ah my dear! This is all very amusing to write about; but to TRANSACT? – god help us well thro' it! (*CL* 17: 210)

What this says is: 'Let me organise my life for your entertainment, and you will repay me with love, attention and letters to which I will reply and through which I will make my life controllable and bearable.' This seems to me to be the constant subtext of Jane's letters to her chosen confidantes.

When Jane writes:

besides I have forgotten in the 'hubbub wild and dire dismay' of late days where I left off in *my life* – that is to say the history of my life – outwardly speaking. (27 Feb. 1847, Huxley 321)

She is equating letter-writing both with her life, and with the history of her life; so her life *is* her letters at the same time as it is also being *recorded* in her letters. The life is made *real* in her letters in a palatable, entertaining way, designed for the recipients' and her own consumption. Thus her created life in her letters becomes a more acceptable reality for her. And this becomes the reality that she has left for us to interpret.

Her relation to Scotland where she lived until she was thirty three and then never lived again was peripheral or at least tangential. Neither she nor Carlyle saw Scotland as the centre of their universe. For Jane it was a land of ghosts, where her parents had lived and died. She writes of a visit to Haddington in August 1849 that she felt like a ghost herself. There is very little in the letters which gives any sense on her part of Scotland or Scottishness. But there is one reported incident of an emotional reaction to one of the great political/religious events of nineteenth-century Scotland: the Disruption in 1843. In July 1843, Jane welcomed at Cheyne Row a young disciple of Thomas's, Francis Espinasse; 'I gave him some tea and what comfort I could', she wrote to Thomas. Espinasse had witnessed in May the great procession of ministers who left the General Assembly of the Church of Scotland to found the Free Church 'for conscience sake . . . Mrs Carlyle declared that if she had been there she would have cried.' (July 1843, *CL* 16: 275)

The Disruption was a great and moving event in Scottish history and Jane may well have genuinely meant this. But it has to be acknowledged that Jane was quite capable of saying it for effect. Espinasse himself may have had some sense of this as he described the rest of the visit thus:

Conversation was soon in full flow, for she knew something of one's Edinburgh belongings, and this was never, in her husband's absence, a silent hostess. The first of her peculiarities which struck me was her Scotch accent . . . as marked as . . . her husband's.

He concluded that she gave 'the impression of a very clever and agreeable woman, with a vein in her both of satire and sentiment.' (*CL*, 16: 276) What Espinasse describes is the way Jane appeared or presented herself in person.

To return to her written self, the remaining question might be: who is she writing for? She is writing for herself, both to define herself and to provide a self-justification for the way she looks at things and for what she is doing with her life. She writes for the correspondent, to entertain, to provide *her* interpretation of her life with Thomas, to impress, to draw the recipient into a collusive interpretation with her of her life. At times she provides a conventionally subversive view of Thomas: for example, speaking of Thomas' yearning for country silence she says: 'as if *that* man *could* enjoy or yet *endure* perfect silence for one week.' (27 Feb. 1849, Huxley 322) She can take the same mildly subversive view of men, or of women's roles. This is the traditional view of the underdog: 'we may not have any power but we have got clarity and knowledge of what the world is really like.' Of course, this view encourages an acceptance of the status quo. Jane may have enjoyed her self-image of a little devilish rebelliousness now and then but, unlike Geraldine Jewsbury, was no real questioner of women's status.

In her letters she consciously invites the reader into a complicity with her interpretation of her life – using the arts of humour, drama, and pathos. The 'reader' is the person she is writing the letter to. But there's a kind of 'generalised recipient' as well, when she makes use of recycled material in near identical form in several consecutive letters. And, because the letters survived, anyone who reads the letters attentively becomes that 'generalised recipient', seduced and cajoled by Jane's rewriting of herself.

The periphery that Jane lived on was that of her husband's career and reputation. What she did in her letters was to centre herself in this periphery, making a triumphant virtue of her situation as a 'genius's' helpmate. The myth may be that she was a great 'missing' novelist. But to lay claim for what she was not seems too reductive of the real power and achievement of what she was. ✿

University of Edinburgh

WORKS CITED

Jane Welsh Caryle's letters to her cousins are in the National Library of Scotland, MS 1893. But, where possible, I have cited Leonard Huxley ed., *Jane Welsh Carlyle: Letters to her Family, 1839–1863* (London, 1924).

C. Ryals, K. J. Fielding, I. Campbell, A. Christianson, H. Smith eds., *The Collected Letters of Thomas and Jane Welsh Carlyle* (Durham, N.C., 1990) Vols. 16 and 17.

Elizabeth Hardwick, *Seduction and Betrayal* (London, 1974).

Mary Poovey, *The Proper Lady and the Woman Writer* (Chicago, 1984).

JAN PILDITCH

Opening the door on Catherine Carswell

When Katherine Mansfield reviewed Catherine Carswell's novel, *Open the Door*, in the *Athenaeum* of June 1920 the review was less than ecstatic. On a personal level this was understandable. In February of that year the consumptive and dying Mansfield received a letter from Carswell's great friend and mentor D. H. Lawrence. It said, among other things, 'You are a loathsome reptile – I hope you will die.'[1] The letter, subsequently destroyed by Mansfield's husband, Middleton Murry, after Lawrence's death, marked the severe but largely inexplicable rift which had occurred in their friendship. This did not prevent the influential Murry from reviewing Lawrence's work in the *Athenaeum* and later in the *Nation*, although his reviews did not satisfy Carswell. For her part, Carswell devoted several pages of *The Savage Pilgrimage*, her biography of Lawrence, to what she called 'Murry's Attack'.

The literary milieu of the day, and the Bloomsbury set in particular, were not renowned for their careful handling of each other's sensibilities, so that it would be a simple matter to put these public denouncements, Mansfield's, Murry's, and Carswell's, down to a mere literary spat. Yet the reviews represent more fundamental differences and take us to the heart of a debate about what constitutes good literature. It is possible to distinguish the influence of culture and gender in the discourse of what purported to be the 'objective' literary judgements of the day, and in view of the widespread influence of the Bloomsbury group, perhaps the time has come to reconsider the place of Carswell's novel not merely in the light of her contemporaries, but in the light of her, and their, cultural and literary judgment.

While endorsing the modernist desirability of objectivity Carswell seems, nevertheless, to have been acutely aware of the differences predicated by her Scottish background. Her championing of the cause of D. H. Lawrence might best be understood in this context. In a review in which Murry denounced an inability to distinguish between the characters of Lawrence's *Women in Love*, he wrote:

We stand by the consciousness and the civilisation of which the literature we know is the finest flower; Mr Lawrence is in rebellion against both . . . He is the outlaw of modern English literature; and he is the most interesting figure in it. But he must be shown no mercy.[2]

If Murry's review was not fulsome with praise nor was it the review of a man bent on revenge for a miserable letter written to his wife. Rather, like his prior rejection of Lawrence's contributions to the *Athenaeum*, it appears to be the result of a difference of opinion as to what constitutes good literature. Murry's designation of Lawrence as a literary outlaw presupposes a common view of the law and civilisation. The law appears to be English, as opposed to Bloomsbury's, in other words national rather than local, and those writing outside of its tenets are to be shown no mercy, especially if they demonstrate ability, presumably, for the common good of literature as a whole. His depiction of Lawrence as 'the most interesting figure' within the English literary scene of the day is at once to recognise his talent, and to marginalise it.

Carswell's novel, *Open the Door*, suffers a like fate at the pen of Mansfield: 'We look in vain' she says of Carswell's Joanna, 'for that precious insight which sets her apart from the other characters and justifies their unimportance.'[3] This review similarly demonstrates a particular, but unspoken, critical standpoint. Following on from Pater, Wilde, and Henry James, Mansfield insists upon the special moment and the special case. It is assumed that Carswell shares this basic tenet of literary excellence but has failed in its execution. Mansfield continues:

All would be well, in fact, if the author did not see her heroine plus, and we did not see her minus. We cannot help imagining how interesting this book might have been if, instead of glorifying Joanna, there had been suggested the strange emptiness, the shallowness under so great an appearance of depth, her lack of resisting power which masquerades as her love of adventure, her power of being at home anywhere because she was at home nowhere.[4]

Mansfield comments on the failure of Joanna to choose to act, as opposed to merely reacting to her circumstances. For Mansfield, this signals a failure of detachment on the part of Carswell. Author and heroine are elided. Joanna's de-racination becomes Carswell's inability to truly ground her character, and the review ends: 'Mrs Carswell has great gifts, but except in her portrayal of Joanna's fanatical mother, she does not try them. They carry her away.'

It is perhaps too much to expect that Mansfield, a New Zealander writing in the 1920's, should understand how far the journey from Glasgow to London can be. Carswell's own thinking in terms of the conflict between 'home' and 'objectivity' can be gauged by her remarks when discussing Mansfield's reaction to Lawrence:

> For a poet born in the Midlands there can be no *recherche du temps perdu* behind soundproof walls while the present goes by to muffled drums outside. The mining Midlands see to that, and I, from Glasgow, understood it, just as Katherine Mansfield from the sweeter home in New Zealand did not. Being herself able to be playful, affectionate, whimsical about 'home' she felt a shade reproachful and superior towards those who could not.[5]

The press of experience which militates against a proper artistic detachment is clearly enunciated by Carswell here on behalf of Lawrence in recognition of a social and cultural undertow. A proper artistic detachment, it is implied, can come about as much from good circumstance as from will, as much from indifference as from control. Ultimately, these comments question the ability of those lacking certain cultural experience to judge the literature of those to whom it is commonplace. The view is prophetically modern and is not uncommon among those excluded from the mainstream of criticism. It is re-iterated in other works by Carswell. In *The Life of Robert Burns* (1930), scathing remarks on Burns' poetry in a contemporary *English Review* draw from Carswell the comment that: 'As London set the fashions, these were sayings to make Edinburgh pause and perpend.'[6] It is a critical position born of Scotland's history that the London educated and domiciled Mansfield was unlikely to understand.

Such views remained an intrinsic part of Carswell's literary being despite her own removal to London, and they offer some clue as to how her problematical first novel might best be read. They imply that it is not enough to find her a place within the tradition of women writers. To plead, for instance, after the manner of feminist criticism, that both Carswell and her heroine Joanna needed a 'room of their own' in order to explain the work is still to miss the point. This is to mark her place within a critical practice and tradition from which, as a Scottish woman writer, she suffered a double exclusion. Carswell did need, as her letters testify, what all women writers of her age needed, the time to write, but she needed more than that. She needed a critical and literary practice which allowed of difference between a novel from London and one from Glasgow, and one which would extend that difference beyond the mere matter of setting and atmosphere. In *Open the Door* Carswell does give us a 'portrait of an artist' as a young woman, but she is, emphatically, a young woman from Glasgow.

Christopher Small has usefully compared Carswell's Joanna with Stephen Dedalus.[7] Joanna, like Dedalus, is an oddity within her own family, but further, in common with other literary heroines of the period she has an inner self which is at odds with social and cultural expectations. Sensitive and intelligent, the young Joanna is aware of the treachery of words. When her mother, overcome by the beauty of the river, infuses the scene with religious intensity: 'They go down to the sea in ships and see His wonders in the mighty deep'[8], Joanna feels merely violated and miserable under the deadening weight of the words. Nevertheless she is aware of a rise of emotion at their beauty. Like Eliot's moonlight the words 'stir memories' and she throws up 'frantic defences against their sympathy'. This ability in words to kindle unbidden emotion threatens Joanna's bid to remain aloof from her mother's fanaticism. Her mother's inner life has long since found vent in religious fervour: 'Without constant and secret prayer she knew herself unable to face the demands of daily life.'(p10) The young Joanna will accept no such safe outlet: 'she was perhaps a changeling'. (p10) Thus Joanna's kinship with the post-Romantic figure of the artist, those detached, creative, and god-like individuals, is established. That this figure presents neither a suitable, nor even a very likely, heroine for a Scottish novel is soon apparent.

Detachment, as Alan Bold has remarked, 'is an unusual quality in Scottish writing.'[9] The long tradition of women's writing in Scotland is no exception.

There, the theme of a divided self, apparent in Hogg, Stevenson, and others, has provided an inescapable backdrop for women writers to play out their concerns. During the nineteenth century English women writers attempted to resolve the dual demands of reason and passion. Charlotte Bronte, in a bid to remain true to social realism in *Villette*, leaves Lucy, not unhappily, in charge of her school when love, passion, and her benefactor are surprisingly lost at sea. In Eliot's *Middlemarch* Dorothea's unhistorical acts transcend the ordinary as we are brought to an appreciation of those on whom 'the growing good of the world is partly dependent'.[10] To imagine Dorothea's suffering can only enhance her heroism. The Scottish Mrs Oliphant's end to *Kirsteen* is more problematical by comparison. Kirsteen, whose true love has died, becomes a successful business woman, saves the Drumcarrow lands, protects the good name of Douglas, and, (like Dorothea) is perhaps a worthy object of universal love and respect. If Kirsteen does not become so it is because the contradictory aspects of this state are too readily apparent in Mrs Oliphant's work:

No one could be more cheerful, more full of interest in all that went on. Her figure had expanded a little like her fortune, but she was the best dressed woman in Edinburgh, always clothed in rich dark-coloured silks and satins, with lace which a queen might have envied. Upon the table by her bed-head there stood a casket, without which she never moved; but the story, of which the records were there enshrined, sometimes appeared to this lady like a beautiful dream of the past, of which she was not always sure that it had ever been.[11]

The casket is all that remains of Kirsteen's passional and sexual self and is too potent a symbol of carefully guarded repression, restriction and waste, to be entirely redeemed by her friendship to the poor and struggling everywhere. Ultimately one is left with the disorderly-order that is provoked by a realistic weighing of contraries, devoid of sentiment, and is epitomised by the good name of Miss Douglas of Moray Place. It is the feminine version of the 'Caledonian antisyzygy' to which Carswell's Joanna is the unfortunate heir.

The theme of the divided self is especially poignant in Joanna who is torn between the Calvinistic sense of the father and the ineffectual religion that has become an excuse for suffering and passivity in her mother. Her father, despite his actual death, lives on, in the long memories of Glaswegians and in dreams. Being allowed to sleep with her mother as a girl brings guilt to Joanna; triggered first by her exhausted mother's refusal to rest, then by the thrill she feels watching her mother undress before finally creeping into her arms: 'in that warm, lovely encircling, her thin little body was flooded with well-being.'(p28) The sense of warmth and well-being is broken by her dream:

Father was dead. They had a cable to say so, had mourned him, and he had no right to come back in this way. In terror, but under a kind of constraint, she opened the door one small inch. And that dreadful stranger who was yet her father tried to push his way into the house.(p28)

In her dream Joanna is overwhelmed by hatred and tries to close the door. On waking the strength of feeling persists: and in that conscienceless moment she decides that 'we can do as we please now he is gone.' But with complete awakening 'all and more than all the repulsion of her dream turned upon herself.'(p29) Surrounded by ineffectual females it is Joanna's father who becomes the keeper of the word. This is a role he assumed literally in life, in view of his possession of the pulpit, but more importantly, it is a role he assumes in the Lacanian sense of entry into a symbolic order. Joanna's female self is associated with the futility associated with the gesture made in order to assuage her conscience: she forces herself to kiss a dirty and blind old woman, who would have preferred a coin dropped in her tin. There is an abundance of conscience, warmth, and well-meaning in the gesture, but in the real world of Glasgow, it is foolish.

Joanna inevitably assumes that her capacity to organise her emotional and intellectual world will hinge upon her capacity to find and marry the right man. Aunt Perdy, who writes to the young Joanna of a 'glorious land of liberty, and sunshine, this refuge of great hearted exiles . . . like dear Byron, like Shelley, and a host of others to whom freedom was life' opens for the young Joanna 'an unsuspected door of escape'.(p85) Aunt Perdy belongs to a fantastic world of dangerous women, but it is a fantastic world which Joanna subjects to homely and realistic detail. She resents the slur on her 'deluded, conventional father' (p85) and on her poor weak mother, and is unimpressed by her Aunt's interest in the Zodiac. Nor is her Aunt entirely free. Her walls are covered with the pictures of the men 'who have made Aunt Perdy what she is' (p137). There is her father, whose ghost comes to her to tell her what words to write; Pulsford, remembered for his *Morgen Rothe*; and Laurence Oliphant. When confronted by the portrait of 'poor Henry' Aunt Perdy retreats into a familiar pattern of religiosity and fantasy:

> I keep his picture there to remind myself that I have forgiven him the great wrong he did me when he put me in a Nursing Home, and kept me locked up there that he might indulge his fleshly lusts with my children's governess . . . I forgave Henry long ago – even before God punished him by a lingering illness . . . I would gladly have nursed him . . . But he refused my offer, and did not even answer my letter of tender forgiveness. In that horrible asylum all those on whom I laid my hands were immediately cured. Thus God causes the wrath of men to praise Him, Joanna. (p138)

This mad woman has perhaps been too long in the attic, and dreams of Papa who comes in sleep and bids her to 'Blot the wicked words of self'. (p143) Yet it is Aunt Perdy who symbolically frees the swallows from the ensnarement of Niccolo and Francesco, and in Carswell's creation of her there is a somewhat peculiar transmutation of Gilbert and Gubar's contention that:

> Even the most apparently conservative and decorous women writers obsessively create fiercely independent characters who seek to destroy all patriarchal structures which both their authors and their author's submissive heroines seem to accept as inevitable.[12]

The destructive impulse marked by Gilbert and Gubar can be recognised in Aunt Perdy's self-righteous contention that God punished her husband by inflicting a long and fatal illness upon him. Such evidence of rebellion, in the nineteenth century, was not projected onto the heroines, but onto some mad or monstrous woman who was then punished in the course of the novel or poem. Thus, according to Gilbert and Gubar 'female authors dramatise their own self division, their desire to accept the structures of patriarchal society and to reject them.'[13]

In Carswell's text the heroine's affinity with the mad woman is clearly established. Joanna looks like Aunt Perdy and shares the same sign of the Zodiac. The dream of Italy proves a palliative against the loss of her dreams about Bob, who Joanna had thought was the right man, so that she can no longer trust her dreams:

Well, you Scottish women with your theories! Tell me what are the things in the world of best worth to a woman! Are they not air, light, gaiety, love, ease, shelter from the brutalities of life, children, tenderness, adoration? Does the freedom you talk of secure you these? Does it not in reality make them impossible?

Mario wins his point. 'It was through her dreams that Bob hurt her. About Mario she had no dreams. He was her escape into reality.' (p100) The notion is not uncommon in women's fiction: Edna Pontellier, in Kate Chopin's *The Awakening*, similarly depicts her inner life as dream, while describing her marriage as an entry into the world of reality. There, as here, the notion signifies an attempt to conform to a social order with which the reality of a largely undefined inner self is completely at odds. As with Edna Pontellier, Joanna's position as the wife of Mario deprives her of all adult freedom and responsibility, but unlike Edna her husband does desire her: 'for beauty he saw in her. She too, like the facade, had a heart for the sun. And he had discovered it.'(p120)

Joanna's 'awakening' takes place within the social and realistic world of marriage which has been incorporated into the dream world of Italy which in turn functions as a signifier for Joanna's inner and sexual self. Thus, after Mario's death, Joanna flees to her other Italian dream, that of a free and independent life. The entire Italian episode, although couched in terms of the fantastic and the unreal, cannot be wholly repudiated. Joanna is divided between the realistic expectations of her Glasgow home and her dream of Italy. The Italian experience is not merely a mistake on Joanna's road to fulfilment, but an intrinsic part of an effort to define and live by an inner female self:

Her life – was it not as that flood? Was it not muddy, littered, unlike the life she would have imagined or chosen? But it was a life. It moved.

It possessed the impulse, the impetus, the inner font of desire – not of mere detached wishes that succeed each other capriciously, but of desire that springs from some undiscoverable source . . . If only she had the courage to obey her true desire always, would she not be purged ultimately of all her falseness?(p187)

The need to be true to the self is apparent here, but equally apparent in the language is the lack of definition and certainty. The amorphous water imagery is itself questioned in the negative, there is a constant redefinition of something, we know not what, from some undiscoverable source, and finally, we are left with again a negative question, without answer. Here there is no determining symbolic order, but rather a feminine emotional spontaneity in which detachment has no place.

Joanna's first attempt to realise her inner self on her return to Glasgow is via the role of daughter – a role reinforced by her Glasgow society and one imbued with guilt: 'And remember my daughter, you will not have your mother with you always. She is growing older, and her constant prayer is that she may not be spared to old age, to be a burden to herself and others.'(p146) Joanna's mother, who manages to exempt her sons from her spiritual passion, nevertheless expects her daughters to follow her religiosity as a means to fulfilment. Her relentless pathos, tied as it is to pulpit and symbolic order, understandably brings Joanna close to despair:

Almost three years now, she had been at home; and it had come to this. She had got no farther than this in fulfilling her dream of daughterhood . . . In practice she could not be the daughter of these dreams. Still less could she be the daughter her mother so passionately wanted. Why was it?(p148)

Joanna had taken refuge from this question in dreams prior to her marriage, but now, 'shaken awake by the vivid physical experience with Mario, she fled outwards to embrace the newly discovered actual . . . She was not merely a woman reprieved, but a woman awakened.'(p148–149) This time she seeks refuge in work, obscurely recognising that her true stimulant lay, not with the praise forthcoming from the outside world, 'but even when it irked her most . . . in the handicap her mother was to her'.(p150) Thus Joanna cannot commit herself wholly to the visual arts, and finds herself unable to 'at all times identify herself with this new, intoxicating, workaday world.'(p149)

The modernist need to become detached in order to produce great art is antithetical to the very impulse which fires Joanna's creativity in the first place, that is her attachment to other and older female members of her family. That family, and Joanna's fricative place within it, is conceived in the context of a city and a nation historically removed from the self-styled centre of cultural and aesthetic judgment. In this way the novel interrogates a central tenet of the modern movement, the need for detachment to produce great art, particularly in relation to the creativity of women. Indeed, Joanna's dalliance with the notion of detachment is, in effect, another fantasy. It is epitomised by her relationship with Pender: 'she and he were under the same spell of helplessness, as if drugged.'(p209)

Pender is perhaps the archetypal artist of the time and is constantly concerned with aesthetics. He is detached, even from his own childhood, and therefore presumably his own past: 'I don't think it particularly interested me being a child.' He is also detached from his own present, living with a wife he doesn't love and with a sense of duty toward his sons which is nebulous at best: 'I shouldn't like to go back on them; or shall we say I haven't yet found anything that seemed to make it worth while doing so?' When Joanna tells him that she loves him he is afraid she is a 'fearful goose', and while she wishes he would take her, he remarks: 'Never mind; this light is very becoming to you my dear . . . In fact you look perfectly lovely to me at this moment.'(p210) Pender's concern with 'the form of the thing' extends into every area of his life, but for as long as he believes in himself, Joanna is content. 'Even to be the toy and the refreshment of one who knew himself to be a creator of beauty was enough.'(p214)

For Joanna Louis Pender represents all that her womanhood and her Scottish nationality have deprived her of:

> For her he personified not only that for which the little green door in the wall of La Porziuncola had stood as the symbol, but also the finely decked luncheon table of Aunt Georgina. And between these two extremes of illicit adventure and conventional elegance (utterly dependent as they are one upon the other) lay the whole wondrous realm which is Society, which is aestheticism, which is history, which is the multi-coloured, solid-seeming fruit of human civilisation. For a complexity of reasons, provincial and individual, the girl had always felt herself deprived of this traditional world. Now in Louis she was to possess it.(p250)

Joanna's deprivations, provincial and individual, mark the double exclusion of a Scottish woman writer. Compare the confident metaphor of Murry writing about Lawrence: 'we stand by the consciousness and the civilisation of which the literature we know is the finest flower'[14] with Carswell's less convinced, and less convincing, 'solid-seeming fruit'.(p250) The consciousness by which Murry stands is also subjective, but it is reflected in the apparently objective reality of social and patriarchal structures, in a given view of history, and in tradition. The economic and political structure of early twentieth century Britain underlies Murry's conviction, just as it undercuts Carswell's authority. Joanna's subjective reality has no external reflectors, and her attempt to realise herself through Louis is doomed to failure. His view of himself is by no means constant, and his view of Joanna subject to flux and change: 'An unfortunate hat . . . could make him, it almost seemed, revise his whole opinion of her.'(p253) He is unable to direct the course of their love, and the fact is borne in upon Joanna that: 'Louis was clutching like a drowning man at her spiritual certainty. It was essentially the same movement as that made thirty years earlier by Sholto her father towards Juley her mother.'(p250) The failure is individual, national, and aesthetic.

Pam Morris has recently, and accurately, used Carswell's novel as an example of the confessional novel, suggesting that Joanna's search for self ultimately becomes a search wholly for sexual fulfilment:

> What she is actually running towards are the arms of the only man who can offer her sexual realisation, who can offer her self. In narrative time this culmination takes place just as the First World War begins; moreover, Joanna's quest for personal space and freedom coincides with the suffragists' struggles which in Glasgow centred on the activities of students and teachers at the College of Art. Her search for her 'self', however, becomes wholly identified with her sexuality.[15]

Yet the importance of Scotland, the past, and the 'outlaw' aesthetic, is so inextricably intertwined with Joanna's progress, that this explanation of the novel's end cannot wholly answer the case. Foucault remarks that:

> The obligation to confess is now relayed through so many different points, is so deeply ingrained in us, that we no longer perceive it as the effect of a power that constrains us; on the contrary, it seems to us that truth, lodged in our most secret nature, 'demands' only to surface.[16]

Foucault is of course writing of a compulsive and internalised need to discover and articulate sexuality, but Joanna's growing awareness of her Scottish heritage is tied so closely to the development of her female and sexual self, that Carswell's novel seems driven by an internalised and equivalent urge to confess, discover, and articulate, her Scottish self, which has been similarly repressed. It is as if Foucault's words applied to Scottish culture and tradition, to nationality as well as sexuality. To be sure Joanna continues to believe herself essentially, and perhaps biologically, excluded from a perceived male capacity to make work a *raison d'être*, although: 'Indeed and indeed men were to be envied in their work.'(p347) She will not, as did her mother, seek resolution in spirituality and suffering; nor can she, given her pragmatic Glasgow setting, walk, like Chopin's Edna Pontellier, into the water. Joanna must find a way of living which incorporates both the fantastic and pragmatic aspects of her being. Her concern cannot rest wholly with one or the other.

Throughout the novel (perhaps typically in a Scottish text), there has lain, behind the fantastic and experimental episodes, a social, and universal reasoning. This, pragmatically, is the need to fall in love with, and to be married to, the right man. In Joanna's case, however, that right man is, and must be, Scottish. It is established early that Urquhart is the right man for he and Joanna can dance together:

> From the outset he caught Joanna up into something of his own dignity . . . Then, as the reel progressed, she began to lose all sense of identity. Every moment she became less herself, more a mere rhythmical expression of the soil from which they both had sprung.

The dance is important. It is a Scottish reel, an art form from which women have never been excluded, and one in which symmetry with one's partner must be undisputed. It is an art form, furthermore, as the Irish Yeats has suggested, in which artist, form, and content are inextricably bound: something which Joanna appears to require in terms of self definition. It is not detachment which Joanna seeks, but yes, a Lawrencian like 'fusion between flesh and spirit in which alone is absolute being.'(p358)

Joanna's self, however, is not endowed upon her by Urquhart: that self must be complete before her final run. Joanna comes to terms first with her father: 'Had he . . . not also been denied fulfilment?'(p334); then with Louis: 'What if the break between them had sprung from his refusal to drag her further into his own long dying?'(p369); and perhaps, most of all, with her own geography, the terrain of her earliest longings. It 'came to her as a perfect astonishment, what she must long before have known, had her childish geography not been of the haziest and never amended – Westermuir lay within twenty miles of Duntarvie.'(p381) At Duntarvie Joanna's Scottish heritage, realised on the train, and her pre-sexual girlhood form a single symbol:

> There it was. There was its perfect circle as of old. There was the living, undespoilable spring that had been set here to spill and spill for ever from its far hidden source in the earth. (p. 389)

It is at this point that Joanna sees that she has been trapped in what is a binary opposition inherent in western thought: 'enfolded in a double mesh of desire . . . each had denied that the other had any right in her . . . both had been needed, that in the following of one alone there would have been sterility.' (p. 390) Without experiencing entrapment, she realises, she could not be free, for freedom lay 'in knowing'. (p. 390) Joanna's recognition of the right man must incorporate this new found knowledge. The dependence of Joanna and Lawrence, then, is equal and mutual, and the perfect circle is defined as love, not sex. In this man Joanna 'knew well that no corner of her life would be – or need ever be – kept from him', so that finally they take the hilly road toward society, toward 'the village' together.

The capacity of love to reconcile opposites is a view which may, ultimately, be termed idealistic, and the ending of the novel could therefore be described as lacking in a social dimension. In Katherine Mansfield's terminology, this may simply be evidence of a lack of control, of Carswell being 'carried away'. But any attempt to redefine relationships between the sexes inevitably abstracts itself to some degree from the social dimension and Carswell was not the only woman of her time to refuse to allow this issue to narrow to the (perhaps simpler) issue of the gaining of the vote. The success of Carswell's text lies with its engagement and participation in the act of breaking down notions of objective value and introducing the difficult negotiation of new kinds of evaluation. Embedded in the honest attempt to define and articulate the Scottish female self lies the subversive act, which is the creation of a cultural space. After all, who would deny her that last flamboyantly female appropriation of the moon, the very symbol of romance, 'like a web of ripe seeds that has this moment been scattered'? ❧

University of Waikato

1   Quoted from: Alpers, Antony, *The Life of Katherine Mansfield*, New York, Viking Press, 1980, p. 310.
2   Coombes, H., ed., *D. H. Lawrence*, (Penquin Critical Anthology) 1973, pp. 138–43.
3   Mansfield, Review.
4   Mansfield, Katherine, Review of *Open the Door, Athenaeum*, 25th June, 1920.
5   Carswell, Catherine, *The Savage Pilgrimage*, Cambridge, Cambridge University Press, 1981, p. 41.
6   Carswell, Catherine, *The Life of Robert Burns*, London, Chatto and Windus, 1930, p. 247.
7   Small, Christopher, 'Engagement and Detachment', *Chapman*, Edinburgh, Autumn/ Winter, 1993, pp. 131–136.
8   Carswell, Catherine, *Open the Door*, London, Virago Press, 1986, p. 10. All future references will be to this edition.

9   Bold, Alan, *Modern Scottish Literature*, London, Longman, 1983, p. 3.

10 Eliot, George, *Middlemarch*, ed. W. J. Harvey, New York, Viking Penquin, 1965, p. 896.

11 Oliphant, Margaret, O. W., *Kirsteen*, intr. Merryn Williams, London, Dent, 1984, p. 342.

12 Gilbert, Sandra M., and Susan Gubar, *The Madwoman in the Attic: The Woman Writer and the Nineteenth Century Imagination*, New Haven, Conn., Yale University Press, 1979, p. 77.

13 ibid. p. 78

14 Coombes, H. pp. 138–43.

15 Morris, Pam, *Literature and Feminism*, Oxford UK and Cambridge USA, Blackwell, 1993, p. 143.

16 ibid, p. 141

Engendered Subjects: subjectivity and national identity in Alasdair Gray's 1982, Janine

In *1982, Janine*, Alasdair Gray's second and, in my view, most successful novel, a crisis of national identity is conflated with a crisis of personal identity through the mental processes of the central protagonist, Jock McLeish. According to Alison Lee, Alasdair Gray's first novel, *Lanark*, is primarily concerned with, 'structures of power, from familial, governmental and corporate control, to the manipulation of the reader and the character'.[1] *1982, Janine* shares these preoccupations of the earlier novel, but in contrast to *Lanark*, which is anchored firmly in the city of Glasgow, *1982, Janine* uses Scotland as a textual site of ideological contest. Gray is one of a long line of writers in Scotland and elsewhere who have merged personal and national narratives in prose fiction – 'nations themselves *are* narrations,' as Edward Said has recently pointed out.[2] However, *1982, Janine* treads a well-worn path only to break down the notion of the romantic hero and undermine romanticised national mythologies. Jock McLeish is a very unexceptional and unhappy man, profoundly insecure in his job and his personal relationships. However, if Jock is a product of his society it is equally valid to say that his society, Scottish society, is a product of him. He is, after all, an example of the proverbial white, middle-class male; a 'Scottish Everyman' as his creator describes him.[3] Several commentators have drawn attention to the social critique of *1982, Janine* but little notice has been paid to the ways in which the text interacts with feminist political discourse. Gray addresses gender-related issues because the gender politics of recent decades makes plainly visible a point at which the personal and political meet. The questions about gender which arise in *1982, Janine* help to contextualise its broad cultural analysis of personal and national identity.

Writing in 1990, Joy Hendry argued in her introduction to the reissue of *Chapman 35–36, 'Scotland: A Predicament For The Scottish Writer?'* that the 'great Scottish success story of the eighties has been the surge of popular interest in all the arts, including literature.'[4] However, at the time of original publication (1983) there appeared little to be optimistic about.

In her original editorial of 1983 Hendry talks of a culture 'being trivialised', of a 'complacent stupor' affecting those involved in Scottish writing, and 'most psychologically damaging of all . . . that sense of powerlessness, which breeds nothing but apathy' (1). The rather bleak picture outlined in Hendry's editorial, echoed by numerous other cultural commentators in the early eighties, can to a large extent be attributed to the aftermath of the failed attempt in 1979 to establish a devolved parliament in Scotland, a campaign to which many of those involved in cultural life had devoted considerable energy. However, 'the Scottish writer' has been assumed to be in a perpetual predicament ever since Edwin Muir published *Scott and Scotland: The Predicament of the Scottish Writer* in 1936. It was the republication of Muir's controversial essay that sparked the *Chapman 35–36* issue in 1983 (after a panel discussion organised by Polygon to launch their new edition of *Scott and Scotland*) but the fact that the essay was republished at this particular time suggests that its argument was all too relevant to cultural debate in the post-1979 fall-out.

Muir's argument that a writer who 'wishes to add to an indigenous Scottish culture and roots himself deliberately in Scotland, . . . will find there, no matter how long he may search, neither an organic community to round off his conceptions nor a literary tradition to support him' (Muir 15), would seem pertinent to debates about cultural authority, links between literature and politics, and the uneasy constitutional position of Scotland in the years immediately after the devolution referendum. Sustaining a debate that has raged fruitlessly since it was fuelled by Hugh MacDiarmid and Edwin Muir in the twenties and thirties might not at first appear a productive critical strategy, yet the challenge Muir offers to 'the Scottish writer' has been interpreted in diverse ways over the last decade: some writers of Scottish formation have taken Muir's argument as a challenge to displace their so-called predicament. *1982, Janine* appeared at a moment when the whole notion of 'the Scottish writer' was being called into question, not just because of the difficulty of defining literature in national terms, but also because the primacy of the author as an agent in literary production had been seriously destabilised by the increasing influence of postmodernist writing and post-structuralist criticism. Arguably, those who attempted to displace the 'predicament of the Scottish writer' succeeded in changing the ground on which the struggle for cultural authority was to be contested in the latter part of the eighties and early nineties. *1982, Janine* seems to have 'captured the mood of the moment' by encapsulating popular progressive nationalist sentiments, narrated from the perspective of a very ordinary Scotsman.

Alasdair Gray's interest in cultural debate about the state of Scottish writing is evidenced by the fact that he was one of five writers who took the platform at the *Scott and Scotland* republication event organised by Polygon. In an article entitled 'A Modest Proposal for By-passing a Predicament'[5] Gray recounts the happenings of that evening in such a way as to diffuse both 'the' predicament of Polygon's public debate, and the indefinite but singular ('a') predicament posed by *Chapman* into a multiplicity of predicaments faced by an unlikely assemblage of writers. I draw attention to this article because Gray's argument therein paves the way for *1982, Janine*; it proffers a helpful avenue of approach not only to the subject matter of the novel, but also to the literary techniques and strategies its author employs.

Describing in retrospect the speech he planned to make, Gray uses the perspective of hindsight to highlight the points at which his plan was open to ridicule. He claims that he intended to avoid personal references, preferring to subsume all particularities into one collective identity of 'the Scottish writer' so that 'the audience would know I was speaking for all of them too' (7). Further, Gray claims he planned to 'paper-over' differences by ignoring

> sexual, parental, educational, religious and emotional predicaments, since these vary from person to person. I would stick to poverty and unemployment, of which everyone has, or pretends to have had considerable experience. In general terms I would explain that The Predicament Of The Scottish Writer is the predicament of the crofter and steelworker – the predicament of Scotland itself. What a radical, hardhitting yet humane speech that would be! Since there would be no crofters or steelworkers in the audience I would not upset a single soul. (7)

Notably, the sexual, parental, educational, religious and emotional predicaments Gray refers to in the quotation above mirror those faced by Jock McLeish, the protagonist of *1982, Janine*.

Gray claims to be unable to remember what he actually said on the occasion in question, but he does recall Iain Crichton Smith speaking 'sadly about the predicament of writing within, and for, the Gaelic and Lowland Scots language groups', Trevor Royle addressing the problems he faced as a Scottish writer having been born in England, Alan Spence talking in terms 'probably as general as my own', and Allan Massie presiding over the affair 'with the crisp firmness of a Victorian schoolmaster'(7). According to Gray, other predicaments became evident during the course of discussion, but most importantly, he describes how he created a new predicament for himself when he rose to the bait of 'a troublemaker [who] tried to get a positive expression of personal prejudice from the platform' by asking why there were no women represented. Gray admits he was stupid to suggest that 'the proportion of male to female writers, statistically calculated, might, er, not, er, perhaps justify, er, the presence of more than half a woman . . .'(7). Gray provides ample evidence in this essay, written subsequently, that he is aware his comments were inappropriate given the quality of writing produced by Scottish women around that time, but by focusing on the vexed question of gender issues, he anticipates the fuller critique of gender politics evident in *1982, Janine* and shows that the predicament arising from the marginal status of women in Scotland is his own predicament also. Gray implies that 'the Scottish writer' is perhaps not as homogenous as some all encompassing theories of his predicament might suggest.

Most relevant of all, however, to *1982, Janine* is Gray's description of how he by-passes his own immediate predicament on the occasion in question. After making his ill-considered comments about women writers, Gray claims that:

> Like a true friend Tom Leonard interrupted me here. He asked if this did not demonstrate that Scottish writing had basically homo-erotic foundation? I was able to change the subject by denouncing him for exposing our secret. Whereupon headmaster dismissed the entire class.(7)

By making a joke about sexuality, Gray is able to avoid Leonard's serious question and simultaneously side-step his own social gaffe. Allan Massie, cast in the role of authority figure, soon puts a stop to their dialogue, which in Gray's account is made to read as childish sexual innuendo. A serious or frank discussion about gender issues or sexuality in relation to Scottish literature could not, it appears, be properly included on cultural or critical agendas. Things have changed somewhat since then, in that the recognition paid to women writers has been greater in the last ten years than in previous decades. *1982, Janine* helps to bridge a path towards less androcentric approaches to literature in Scotland. Gray's article, in which he goes on to argue that 'the fact that Scotland is governed from outside itself, governed against the advice of the three Parliamentary Commissions and against the wishes of most Scots who voted on the matter, cannot be used to explain our lack of talent because that lack is no longer evident'(9), sets the context for *1982, Janine*. Indeed, the novel is perhaps most helpfully viewed as 'an *im*modest proposal for by-passing a predicament' as it is a confident and stylish attempt to unearth and uproot cultural identity in many of its manifestations in order to cultivate a flourishing and inclusive national consciousness. In *1982, Janine*, Gray brings Jock to a more secure sense of personal identity by problematising his protagonist's subjectivity.

It has become commonplace for literary critics to argue that the meanings of literary texts are mediated, provisional, and unstable, but some feminist thinkers, amongst others, pay particular attention to the role of literature as a propagator of political power: as Gayatri Spivak contends, 'the role of literature in the production of cultural representation should not be ignored'.[6] Catherine Belsey, in her influential essay 'Constructing the Subject: Deconstructing the Text', traces the origins of consciously political literary criticism to Althusser's analysis of 'ideological state apparatuses'. Belsey's own main concerns are with representations of women in fiction and the status of women involved in the production of literature, and she uses Althusser to support her argument that literature not only 'represents the myths and imaginary versions of social relationships which constitute ideology, but also that classic realist fiction, the dominant literary form of the nineteenth century and arguably the twentieth, 'interpellates' the reader, addresses itself to him or her directly, offering the reader as the position from which the text is most 'obviously' intelligible, the position of the subject in (and of) ideology' (Belsey 593). Alison Lee argues that, 'In *Lanark*, the tyranny of the visual image as a mimetic device is paralleled in the exploration of structures of power'(99). She contends that, 'while *Lanark* provides a critique of representation, it does so by virtually enacting the very power that is thematized and criticized in the novel'(114). Lee's analysis of *Lanark* is equally applicable to *1982, Janine* where the crisis of representation centres not just upon the way in which 'the nation' is perceived, but more radically, on the way in which human subjectivity itself is defined, and the ways in which it is constructed within ideology.

It is no coincidence that feminists like Spivak and Belsey have been at the forefront of critical attempts to change notions of what constitutes subjectivity: a great deal of Western history has presented women as passive objects rather than active agents. By uncovering the assumptions at the heart of such representations, feminists have attempted to change women's social positions during the course of the twentieth century. If a key tactic of the women's movement in the US and UK during the seventies was to convince women that 'the personal is political', the maxim could equally be applied to the process by which Jock McLeish becomes aware of his own position in relation to the forces and institutions that influence his life. Just as women were encouraged to use their new-found knowledge of their bodies and their social position to make decisions based on their own best interests and desires, so too Jock McLeish is able to free himself from some of the more adversely determining influences on his life once he becomes aware of the cultural and institutional forces that impede his moral choices. The sources of Jock McLeish's entrapment are dissected in *1982, Janine* in order to liberate him from their effects.

By drawing a parallel between the political strategies of the women's movement, feminist literary criticism and the literary tactics of Alasdair

Gray I enter a potentially controversial area of critical debate, yet one which has yet to be thoroughly addressed in relation to *1982, Janine*. The novel's central metaphor compares Scotland's political situation to that of an abused woman; some readers have considered the book's literary depictions of women to be 'pornographic'. Throughout *1982, Janine* Gray uses explicit language and sexual images to make a clear connection between the personal and political, but the following extract is a particularly stark example:

> But if a country is not just a tract of land but a whole people then clearly Scotland has been fucked. I mean that word in the vulgar sense of *misused to give satisfaction or advantage to another*. Scotland has been fucked and I am one of the fuckers who fucked her and I REFUSE TO FEEL BITTER OR GUILTY ABOUT THIS. I am not a gigantically horrible fucker, I'm an ordinary fucker. And no hypocrite. I refuse to deplore a process which has helped me become the sort of man I want to be: a selfish shit but a comfortable selfish shit. (136–37)

Jock confronts his own complicity in what he sees as a process of exploitation, but resists the nagging of his conscience to alter his attitudes or behaviour. At a later stage in the novel Jock makes a specific correlation between the nature of his day-to-day work as a security installations supervisor and his relationships with women. Jock, whose technological skills have been utilised to supervise the security installations at nuclear shelters within Scotland, takes stock of the militarisation of Scotland during the Cold War and the economic decline of Clydeside. Jock tells himself that 'since the American polaris base arrived in the fifties capital has withdrawn and manufacture concentrated in the south. I am sure there is no connection between these two events'(136), but later, his reasoning forces him to denounce the proliferation of the nuclear arms race as a sterile and morally bankrupt exercise, precisely because he makes a mental connection between the power relations operating in his personal sex-life and the power relations operating between nations:

> Everyone wanted the moon until one day a great nation became wealthy enough to woo her. So scientists and technicians went pimping to this great nation and got rich by selling a quick moonfuck . . . and now nobody wants the moon. She holds nothing human but shattered rockets and rundown machines that litter her crust like used contraceptives proving that Kilroy was here. The moon is still a dead world and nightly reminder that technological men are uncreative liars, mad gardeners who poison while planting and profit by damaging their own seed, lunatics who fuck and neglect everything in reach

which has given them strength and confidence, like . . . like . . . (Like Jock McLeish fucking and neglecting Denny for a woman he could not fertilise.) (312–13)

In emphasising the way in which the international arms race abuses the planet, Jock also draws attention to the fact that his 'very ordinary' treatment of Denny is damaging. It is important to re-emphasise that the alignment of the national and the individual, political and personal is sustained throughout the novel. However, even though it is possible to view Gray's wide-ranging social criticisms as criticisms of patriarchal power structures, there are some difficulties in accepting *1982, Janine* as a feminist tract. The novel does contain disturbing images which emanate from a view of women which feminists (of both genders) have sought to dispel. Jock McLeish's assertion that 'nowadays Britain is OF NECESSITY organised like a bad adolescent fantasy'(139) makes *1982, Janine* a confrontational book. Of course, Jock is a fictional character, and Gray encourages his readers to put some distance between Jock's opinions, his own authorial opinions, and their individual opinions by warning that the novel 'is full of depressing memories and propaganda' (back cover). Gray also explicitly distances himself from Jock in the Epilogue ('Though Jock McLeish is an invention of mine I disagree with him'[345]) but he suggests that by becoming involved with Jock's narrative and participating in Jock's 'bad adolescent fantasies' readers are also implicated in the process of exploitation. For many pro-feminist readers this may be an alienating and upsetting process, even though Gray is equating sexual with economic and political oppression. If Jock's fantasies are found distasteful or offensive, the political strategies with which Jock explicitly associates them can be viewed in an equally dim light, but if, on the contrary, Jock's fantasies are found enjoyable or exciting – if readers identify with Jock – then those readers are challenged to reassess their own attitudes and values as the novel unfolds. Is Alasdair Gray justified in presenting such negative images of women, even if his intent or effect (neither of which can be easily ascertained) is to undermine the potency of those images? Or do the images of Janine, Superb, Big Momma and Helga (Jock's fantasy figures) merely perpetuate offensive stereotypes? There is no simple or single answer to these questions, but the political allegory of *1982, Janine* relies on readers being shocked by the fantastic images and sexual brutality inside Jock's mind. If the images of these women are seen as normal and acceptable, the social and political system which is destroying Jock can also be seen as palatable. In order to render the text 'obviously intelligible' (to borrow Belsey's term) readers must identify with Jock McLeish and must adopt the subject position of Gray's drunken insomniac. As every reader becomes the site of literary production, every reader who looks at Jock creates a stake for her or himself in the novel's process of representation.

Yet Gray cannot control the reception of his novels, even if he can point his readers in certain directions, and the two reading strategies I outline above are only two of a multitude of possible responses to *1982, Janine*. The novel itself may not be internally consistent any more than readers are consistent in their reading practices. Some insight into the problem of defining subjectivity and the equally problematic question of how textual meaning is constructed in relation to gender is offered by Mary Jacobus.[7] Jacobus argues 'the production of sexual difference can be viewed as textual, like the production of meaning . . . In order to read as women we have to be positioned as already-read (and hence gendered)'(945). She continues:

> The monster in the text is not woman . . . ; rather it is this repressed vacillation of gender or the instability of identity – the ambiguity of subjectivity itself which returns to wreak havoc on consciousness, on hierarchy, and on unitary schemes designed to repress the otherness of femininity.(945)

Jacobus makes it clear that 'reading as a man must involve a similarly double or divided demand'(949); relating her argument to *1982, Janine* it becomes evident that Gray's work demands a reconsideration of gender roles in the construction of personal identity.

Jock's identity is most strongly rooted in his work, in his childhood experiences of school and family, and in his intimate relationships with women. Few of Jock's life experiences are very positive; those that are have been transient. Jock, thinking back to the high point of his adult life, his relationship with a loving but unsophisticated girl called Denny, describes his destructive behaviour and disregard for her feelings as 'terrible stuff, very ordinary and very terrible'(23). Jock certainly treats Denny badly, but he is not physically abusive towards her or any of the other 'real' women in his life. His fantasies, however, detail rape and other forms of physical violence perpetrated against imaginary women who have counterparts in Jock's past. Alasdair Gray's so-called 'pornographic' figures are clearly related to their naturalised fictional counterparts. Jock can only gain pleasure from his imaginary world by persuading himself that, 'there is NO CONNECTION AT ALL'(53) between his mother and Big Momma, and by listing 'IMPORTANT DIFFERENCES BETWEEN SUPERB AND MY FORMER WIFE'(33). The women in Jock's life, like Jock himself, are all portrayed within a broad social framework which emphasises their agency as well as their powerlessness. Helen, for example, has lied to Jock (and her other lover) and tricked him into marrying her. Jock positions himself in a feminine role in relation to Helen, reversing the notion of women as 'passive victims within patriarchy': he wonders if he can explain to Helen's father that 'his daughter had used me like a whore, discarded me and then proposed marriage'(297). Jock is bitter about the circumstances of his marriage, which is why he can justify imagining Helen as Superb and enjoy subjecting her to various tortures. Within the context of some nasty domination fantasy, Jock is able to conclude 'When we consider how the winners shaft the losers, the strong shaft the weak, the rich shaft the poor, accusations of sex-discrimination are irrelevant. Most men are poor weak losers. Many women are not'(121). Jock McLeish attempts to empower himself by exercising control over others – something he can only do in his mind. His agency is concentrated in his imagination and in his ability (which he shares with Gray in the role of author) to construct and present women as he pleases. As the novel develops Jock's perspective and opinions undergo thorough revision and transformation. Indeed, the narrative is driven by Jock's need to realise a secure sense of identity which does not depend on the domination or exploitation of others.

Critics sympathetic to *1982, Janine* have felt it necessary to defend its contents. Marshall Walker's second reference to the novel in his essay 'The Process of Jock McLeish and the Fiction of Alasdair Gray'[8] describes it as 'the anti-pornographic *1982, Janine*'(38). Christopher Harvie,[9] too, is slightly apologetic, arguing that the novel, '*despite its obsessions and perversions*, ends with a distinct if tentative sense of optimism'(83) [my emphasis]. Since the 'trial of Lady Chatterley' in 1959, literary forms of explicit representation have been increasingly available. Most of the contemporary political debate about sexually graphic material has centred on visual, not literary representations, and the extent to which legal sanction should be exercised over their production and distribution.[10] Arguably, there is a great deal more graphic imagery in fiction produced for mass markets (often oriented towards women) – and certainly no fewer sexist assumptions – than in *1982, Janine*. However, even well-informed and reasonable commentators have argued that 'a novel or a painting should not be exempted as pornography because the white male literary establishment calls it art'[11](Itzin, 452). *1982, Janine* attracted controversy upon publication because of its 'pornographic' content. Gray assimilated early reviews into a three-page 'Criticism of the Foregoing' at the end of the paperback edition. The comments range from 'Radioactive hogwash' (Peter Levi) to J. A. McArdle's assessment that the novel is 'a thoughtful and sad study of the human predicament; to be trapped in a world where the little man, woman or country will always be exploited by the big bullies.' Gray juxtaposes positive and negative reviews against each other, emphasising the seemingly contradictory responses of the literary style-setters of the press: Paul Ableman suggests that Gray's prose style could be 'refined and strengthened' while

William Boyd, in the very next excerpt, argues: 'His style is limpid and classically elegant.' In actual fact, it seems that all the reviewers, even those who deprecate the novel, make pertinent points – they are all right and consistent within their own frames of reference. Whilst mocking journalistic review styles, the inclusion of review snippets also serves to illustrate that meaning is determined by readers' preconceptions, however hard an author may try to exert her or his influence. Gray's readers are strongly encouraged to make up their minds for themselves, not only about his book, but about all the moral and political questions it raises. The 'advertisement', then, provides useful access to the source of *1982, Janine*'s controversy.

Alasdair Gray invites his readers to become voyeurs in Jock's mental landscape; a landscape which contains depictions of women similar to those found in the mass-produced erotic magazines sold by every newsagent. Any discomfort caused by the depictions of Janine, Superb, Big Momma, and Helga is heightened by the fact that few if any readers can come to the book innocent of its sexual content. Readers are well-warned on the back-cover that the novel is 'mainly a sadomasochistic fetishistic fantasy,' and the Table of Contents explains that Chapter Two is 'a recipe for pornography and political history'. Following the success of *Lanark*, *1982, Janine* was widely reviewed upon publication;[12] no-one need be in any doubt before entering Jock's imagination that there are likely to be, depending on individual preferences, a few shocks and thrills along the way. Yet there seems to be a certain queasiness and reticence surrounding discussions of sexuality in Scottish literary criticism, in sharp contrast to the subject matter of many of the most lauded fictions of this century. Voyeurism and sexual fantasy are not new in Scottish fiction, as Stephen Boyd points out[13], but unlike Tam o' Shanter, Jock McLeish is, in a sense, a professional voyeur. He is a supervisor by trade, and of security installations. Gray breaches the security systems of social propriety not only by exposing Jock's sexual fantasies, but also by implicating his readers. This observation adds weight to the point made earlier that whether we identify ourselves as readers looking into Jock's mind or allow ourselves to identify with Jock the textual subject we become implicated in his world.

Scopophilia is arguably a more important component in the reading of *1982, Janine* than other conventional sources of textual pleasure. Stephen Boyd is the only critic to have drawn more than passing attention to the cinematic aspects of the novel, despite the fact that from the outset the temporally and geographically specific location of the novel, Scotland in 1982, is juxtaposed to the remote and materially unconstituted terrain of Hollywood.[14] *1982, Janine* uses cinematic techniques as literary devices: the novel's fantasies are (rather self-reflexively) constructed as a cinematic narrative, and readers are positioned as viewers. Good evidence for such a reading is provided by the explicit cinematic references made in relation to Helga, who in Jock's fantasies is a film director. Jock says, 'Helga is crucial, she brings all the other girls together' and tells himself he must 'get back to Helga in the viewing theatre'(157). More importantly, Gray creates a literary montage effect by 'switching scenes' from Jock's historical memories to his ahistorical fantasies. Although Janine's opening scene is repeated again and again ('Janine is worried and trying not to show it . . .'[12]) its meaning is unstable. The novel is 'cut' like a film which returns to this same image of Janine in such a way as to emphasise how its significance changes as the novel progresses. When Jock's sexual fantasies are thought of as a cinematic text of moving, changing images, it becomes quite clear that the novel is an assault on the politics of the voyeuristic gaze, and that the widescreen of the reader's mind is where the action and conflict are situated. Describing how scopophilia (a less loaded term than voyeurism) can operate in cinematic representations, Laura Mulvey (from Freud) associates 'pleasure in looking' with 'taking other people as objects, subjecting them to a controlling and curious gaze'(434). The act of looking does not necessarily always imply control, but certainly Jock's women become 'objectified others'(434) within the terms of Mulvey's definition, because Jock is director of his own imagination. Jock in turn is subjected to his reader's controlling consciousness. Mulvey also highlights another aspect of scopophilia relevant to *1982, Janine* – 'its narcissistic aspect' which 'comes from identification with the image seen' (435). Mulvey argues that 'the voyeuristic-scopophilic look that is a crucial part of traditional filmic pleasure can be broken down'(441) by exposing the structure of 'the gaze' and upsetting its conventions. Alasdair Gray, I want to argue, actually breaks down both visual conventions and narrative expectations in his cinematic literary text by upsetting Jock's, and by extension the reader's, subjectivity. To put it simply, Jock *is* Janine. Recounting his early sexual fantasies (which involved Hollywood film stars) Jock remembers 'telling myself stories about a very free attractive greedy woman who, confident in her powers, begins an exciting adventure and finds she is not free at all . . . The woman is corrupted into enjoying her bondage and trapping others into it. I did not notice that this was the story of my own life. I avoided doing so by insisting on the *femaleness* of the main character'(193).[15] Gray merges the identity of protagonist and victim so that by the end of the novel Jock can say 'Oh Janine, my silly soul, come to me now'(341). The process of Janine's development shows Gray breaking down fixed categories of representation. Janine eventually becomes an active agent in her own narrative, but only when Jock realises that he too has some agency: 'Hell no! Surprise them. Shock them. Show them more than they ever expected to see'(341), decides Janine. Janine's liberation is sexual because sexuality has been the source of her disempowerment.[16] Jock is able to gain a new perspective on his own sexuality – his 'problem'(12), as he perceives it – by uncovering the ways in which it has been constructed. Gray uses graphic and discontinuous images to expose profitably the political implications of gender and subject construction. Jock and his creator move into close proximity when Jock describes how he abandoned Denny:

> Only horror films and fairy-stories tell the truth about the worst things in life, the moments when hands turn into claws and a familiar face becomes a living skull. My words turned a woman into a thing and I could not face the thing I had made because the thing saw in my face the disgust it caused me. (244)

However, key questions posed in relation to Alasdair Gray's use of 'bad adolescent fantasy' have often been framed in moral terms: does the existence of sexual exploitation, in particular the sexual and social marginalisation of women in the material world, justify the reproduction of oppressive images, even where the intent (in so far as intent can be established) is to undermine the prevailing social assumptions that give rise to it? Gray would seem to think so. *1982, Janine* presents itself as a novel within a literary tradition of social dystopia. Orwell's *1984*, originally published in 1948, enjoyed an enormous reappraisal in the year to which its title alluded – also the year in which *1982, Janine* appeared. Apart from cashing in on the titular association *1982, Janine*, in contrast to Orwell's novel, projects backwards into history to interpret the present, rather than using a futuristic vision. An epigraph on the cover of the first edition of *1982, Janine* reads: 'Truly the remedy's inside the disease and the meaning of being ill is to bring the eye to the heart'(Alan Jackson). Gray paints a bleak picture of the present in order to emphasise that the social malaise Jock McLeish perceives in Scottish society is made manifest in his personal experiences. The metaphor can be reversed too: Jock's own 'degeneracy' (he keeps his sadomasochistic fantasies and his political preferences secret because he suspects they are socially unacceptable) is symbiotically related to social decay. Jock is indeed 'cured' in *1982, Janine*, at least partially, but to bring Jock to self-knowledge requires Gray to intrude upon the most private corners of Jock's mind.

Gray's linkage of individual to social or national concerns is hardly a new development in fiction, and amongst numerous writers of the Victorian era who sought to draw attention to social injustice through the portrayal of poverty and human suffering in their fiction Dickens has had a particularly strong influence on Gray. If two of the great social ills of the eighties were the nuclear arms race and gender inequality, Gray is far from original in considering them appropriate subject matter for fiction. The question remains unanswered, however, why the sexual content of *1982, Janine* has been considered more shocking than Gray's warnings of nuclear holocaust. The answer lies in several areas. Foucault, following Althusser's considerations of ideology, has demonstrated that the very architectural designs used for prisons, schools, and hospitals carry powerful assumptions about the nature and purpose of their respective forms of social organisation.[17] It is those parts of ideology most widely disseminated – what is thought of as 'normal' or even 'natural' – where the operation of power is least contested. In *The History of Sexuality* Foucault explores in some depth ways in which sexuality operates as a powerful ideological discourse in Western society. The attraction of Foucault's thought for many feminists lies in his 'exposure' of the ideological discourses governing social institutions; institutions (like church, government, work practices, the academy, marriage) which have traditionally subordinated women. Foucault's thought has been instrumental in changing the ways in which society is understood. For many contemporary feminist thinkers, society is now better understood in terms of its organising structures than solely in terms of the individuals comprising it, irrespective of gender.

Given the history of the women's movement and the fact that women's bodies have been seen as a site of ideological contest over a considerable period of time, it becomes easy to see why 'second wave' feminists, many of whom were well-educated and financially secure, and many of whom were for the first time in a position to control their fertility, reasoned that the physical restraints placed on women had been far more instrumental in maintaining gender discrimination than had educational or economic factors. Andrea Dworkin, a leading figure in feminist politics since the seventies, places great emphasis on the centrality of sexual imagery in the oppression of women: 'At the heart of the female condition is pornography: it is the ideology that is the source of all the rest; it truly defines what women are in this system.'[18] More recently she has argued: 'Equality for women requires remedies for pornography, whether pornography is central to the inequality of women or only one cause of it'.[19] However, Dworkin continues to maintain that 'the oppression of women occurs through sexual subordination'(526).[20] Jock McLeish might well agree. Twice in *1982, Janine* Jock confides that his 'problem is sex'(12 & 16), the second time adding the proviso that 'if it isn't, sex hides the problem so completely that I don't know what it is.' Arguably, the weakness of Dworkin's thesis lies in the fact that she considers pornography a *cause* of gender inequality. There is no reason to suppose that sexually graphic metaphors or images are any more effective in shaping negative attitudes towards women than non-sexual ones, despite extensive research which has attempted to prove causal links. In the course of *1982, Janine*, Jock discovers that his sexual problems are symptomatic of his moral problems, and that those are rarely matters of private morality, but more often of social morality.

The second problem with criticism of *1982, Janine* on the grounds of its so-called 'pornographic' content is that pornography is particularly hard to define. Gloria Steinem has tried to differentiate between 'erotica' and 'pornography', but as there is no legal definition of either, the distinction becomes, as Ellen Willis puts it, 'what I like is erotica, and what you like is pornographic'.[21] One point on which both Dworkin and leading anti-censorship campaigner Gayle Rubin agree is that 'erotica is simply high class pornography'.[22] Those who attempt to argue that pornography is 'sexist and violent by definition' find themselves in a tautological position, whereby 'pornography' 'by definition cannot be reformed'(Rubin 27) but remains as difficult to characterise as before. Ironically, such definitions would probably exclude a great deal of 'hard-core' porn where women are shown as equal and willing participants, or even in a position of dominance. To define porn as material which 'demeans or degrades' women also falls into the trap of assuming that all women are degraded and demeaned by the depiction of certain acts. For Laura Kipnis the danger of pornography lies in its

> hypostatizing [of] female sexuality and assigning it to all wom-
> en [which] involves universalizing an historically specific class
> position . . . not as something acquired and constructed through
> difference, privilege, and hierarchy, but as also somehow inborn – as
> identical to this natural female sexuality (381).

Unfortunately, many arguments decrying pornography fall into the same trap of adopting a universalising view of women. This is not to say that certain images are anything other than extremely offensive within the particular context of contemporary Scottish society, but Kipnis's observation makes it difficult to argue that *1982, Janine* is 'pornographic' without also subscribing to an objectifying view of women or reading the novel highly selectively by focusing only on the fantasy scenes. By contrast, Alasdair Gray, as I have already demonstrated, specifically connects Jock's female sex objects to naturalised women, whose material circumstances he is careful to detail.

By describing *1982, Janine* as 'pornographic', Alasdair Gray also positions his novel within the terms of a specific contemporary feminist debate. Gayle Rubin points out that 'pornography in the contemporary sense did not exist before the late nineteenth century' when it 'was coined *from Greek roots* . . . when many of the sex terms still in use (such as homosexuality) were assembled from Greek and Latin root words'(35). Rubin, who attempts to give a historical context to the debate, argues that pornography can be considered as a central component in the condition of women only if it 'is conceptualized as a trans-historical category' (35). For Rubin, the term 'embodies not the prejudices of the Greeks, but those of the Victorians'. However, even if Gray's use of the word 'pornography' alludes to the Victorian values the novel seeks to debunk and Victorian inhibitions it seeks to dispel, the issue at stake remains whether or not he is justified in his use of explicit imagery. It is possible that the 'message' given by, for example, the image of Superb tied-up against her will, yet sexually aroused (55), is in direct conflict with the textual 'message' that women are hurt by exploitative behaviour.[23] Rubin offers evidence that there is 'no systematic correlation between low status for women and cultures in which sexually explicit visual imagery exists, and high status for women and societies in which it does not'(35), despite extensive research attempting to establish such a correlation. However, Gray's fiction as a whole teaches that standards of decency are important to our society and that society collectively and individually is responsible for supervising its own 'security installations'. Perhaps it is a hangover of Victorian concepts of morality in contemporary Scottish culture that has caused critical consternation about *1982, Janine*. Whatever conclusions individual readers might draw, it is clear that the ideal of Victorian femininity is well-served by the notion that all sexual images are morally suspect, and that women who exercise sexual agency are somehow 'unnatural'. By contrast, by contextualising gender issues within a broad framework of social concerns in *1982, Janine*, Gray not only displays his own feminist sympathies, he also places gender-related issues at the centre of Scottish cultural debate.

University of Glasgow

BIBLIOGRAPHY

Belsey, Catherine 'Constructing the Subject: deconstructing the text' (1985) in Warhol & Herndl, eds. pp. 593–619.

Boyd, Stephen 'Black Arts: *1982 Janine* and *Something Leather*' in Crawford & Nairn, eds.

Crawford, R. & Nairn, T. *The Arts of Alasdair Gray* Edinburgh: Edinburgh University Press, 1991.

Dworkin, Andrea 'Against the Male Flood: Censorship, Pornography and Equality' in Itzin ed. pp. 515–535.

Foucault, Michel *Discipline and Punish* (1975) trans. Alan Sheridan. London: Penguin Books Ltd., 1979.

——*The History of Sexuality: Volume I, An Introduction* (1976) Trans. Robert Hurley. London: Penguin Books Ltd., 1979.

Gray, Alasdair *Lanark: A Life in Four Books* Edinburgh: Canongate Publishing Ltd., 1981.
——*1982, Janine* London: Jonathan Cape, 1984.
——*1982, Janine* Middlesex: Penguin Books Ltd., 1985.
Hendry, Joy ed. *Chapman 35–36* Reprint, 1990.
Itzin, Catherine ed. *Pornography: Women Violence and Civil Liberties, A Radical New View* Oxford: Oxford University Press, 1993.
Jacobus, Mary 'Reading Women (Reading)' (1987) in Warhol & Herndl, eds. pp. 944–960.
Kipnis, Laura '(Male) Desire and (Female) Disgust: Reading Hustler' *Cultural Studies* ed. Grossberg, Nelson & Treicher. London and New York: Routledge, 1992.
Lee, Alison *Realism and Power: Postmodern British Fiction* London and New York: Routledge, 1990.
Muir, Edwin *Scott and Scotland: The Predicament of the Scottish Writer* (1936) Folcroft, Pa: Folcroft Library Editions, 1971.
Mulvey, Laura 'Visual Pleasure and Narrative Cinema' (1975) in Warhol & Herndl eds. pp. 432–442.
Rubin, Gayle 'Misguided, Dangerous, and Wrong' *Bad Girls and Dirty Pictures: The Challenge to reclaim Feminism* ed. Assiter & Carol. London: Pluto Press, 1993.
Said, Edward *Culture and Imperialism* London: Vintage, 1993.
Spivak, G. C. 'Three Women's Texts and a Critique of Imperialism' (1985) in Warhol & Herndl eds. pp. 798–814.
Warhol, R. & Herndl, D. P. eds. *Feminisms: an anthology of literary theory and criticism* New Brunswick, New Jersey: Rutgers University Press, 1991.

NOTES

1   Lee, p. 100.
2   Said, p. xiii.
3   Personal interview, January 1994.
4   Editorial, *Chapman 35–36* Reprint.
5   *Chapman 35–36*, p. 7–9.
6   Spivak, p. 798.
7   In 'Women Reading (Women)' (1987).
8   In Crawford and Nairn, eds.
9   In Crawford and Nairn, eds.
10   Current debate centres on television violence and the wide availability of videos which depict explicit sex and violence. During the 1980s support for campaigns to remove erotic magazines from High Street newsagencies was widespread amongst feminists.
11   Catherine Itzin, 'Pornography and Civil Liberties: Freedom, Harm and Human Rights' in Itzin, ed.
12   Graphic excerpts from *1982 Janine* also appeared in *Cencrastus*, April 1983, prior to the novel's publication.
13   'Black Arts' in Crawford and Nairn, eds.
14   'Black Arts' in Crawford and Nairn, eds.
15   Gray cites the classic french film *Belle de Jour*, wherein an attractive, financially secure young married woman becomes a prostitute, as one of his sources in the epilogue of *1982, Janine*.

16   Those who challenged the social position of women during the eighteenth and nine-teenth centuries usually grounded their arguments in notions of individual subjectivity and demanded equal rights for women and men. However, Simone de Beauvoir in *The Second Sex* (1959) demonstrated forcefully ways in which women's bodies have been commodified within Western society: women's sexuality being bought and sold within the institution of marriage, and denied expression within mainstream Western religious traditions.

17   Foucault, *Discipline and Punish*.

18   *Right-Wing Women* Perigee, New York, 1983. Quoted in Assiter & Avedon, 34.

19   'Against the Male Flood', Itzin, 533.

20   Dworkin's views are often misrepresented or taken out of context. She is less of an essentialist than some of her critics suggest, and her arguments have undergone considerable development over time, as the quotations above demonstrate.

21   Quoted by Gayle Rubin, p. 28.

22   Andrea Dworkin, quoted in Rubin, p. 164.

23   Laura Kipnis uses the example of a notorious *Hustler* cover which depicted 'a woman being ground up in a meat grinder'(385) with the caption 'We will no longer hang woman up as pieces of meat' to illustrate the way in which conflicting meanings can be constructed ('Reading Hustler' Grossberg, et al.).

The Scottish Ancestor: a Conversation with Alice Munro

Chris Gittings: You mentioned that you are moving. Does packing up things and leaving a house knock loose any stories?

Alice Munro: (laughter) Listen I never need something to (laughter) knock loose stories. If I could just live long enough to do what I've got in my head I'll be lucky. I mean it's never a problem with me to get ideas, it's how to work the ideas into what I want that is the big problem.

Chris Gittings: When I met you in Glasgow we discussed very briefly your Scottish ancestry, and your interest in the Scottish influence on Canadian culture.

Alice Munro: Yes.

Chris Gittings: When did you first become aware of this influence and how important is it to your writing?

Alice Munro: You know I wasn't aware of it at all when I was growing up because my family never talked about history, or ancestors, or anything, and I didn't know much about this. And, of course I lived in the kind of community where you don't think much about what the community is like you just think the whole country is like this because there weren't many people coming in from outside, and we didn't go out, and so it's only when you move away that you begin to define the community you grew up in, or to think about ways in which it's unique or interesting.

Chris Gittings: So, was it later in life when you started writing, and writing about that community, that you started to recognize this Scottish influence?

Alice Munro: Quite a bit later, actually. Yeah when I started to write about the community but then I was at first just writing about what I found in it, you know, and then much later probably as I became middle aged and around the time my father died I started getting these feelings of – and many people do. I think that the time for ancestors seems to be late middle age; you find all these people going around, you know, checking the records . . .

Chris Gittings: Like Hazel.

Alice Munro: Yes, exactly (laughter), and so I started to get very interested because then I found to my surprise that the poet Hogg was a connection. James Hogg's mother was the sister of my direct ancestor, do you see? So his grandfather was my direct ancestor.

Chris Gittings: Yes; he got all of those wonderful ballads from his mother.

Alice Munro: He did, yes! I mean that really fascinates me because I could see this kind of thing in the family, the urge to, uh, there's this terrific feeling to be practical, but underneath there's this kind of thing about, uh, well, I could see that she would be a collector of ballads; that would fit in.

Chris Gittings: People like Scott appropriated them or recorded them for her . . .

Alice Munro: But she didn't like that.

Chris Gittings: No, things become fixed and lose the energy of orality.

Alice Munro: She said 'They'll never be sung more.'

Chris Gittings: Do you read contemporary Scottish fiction at all?

Alice Munro: Well, you know, I don't get much of it. I'd like to, but I haven't really. What should I be reading? The writer I know is the poet Liz Lochhead and I like her stuff and, uh, who else should I read?

Chris Gittings: Have you run across Janice Galloway at all?

Alice Munro: No.

Chris Gittings: She's a fairly new face on the Scottish literary scene. She has published a collection of short stories, *Blood*, and a novel, *The Trick is to Keep Breathing*.

Alice Munro: I'll remember that because when I was looking at stuff when I was over there I seemed to find there was a dearth of women writers.

Chris Gittings: Did you come across Naomi Mitchison at all?

Alice Munro: I know about her, yes. I don't think I've read anything.

Chris Gittings: Like yourself she is interested in family history and juxtaposes herself and World War II Scotland to her ancestors and Scotland following the Jacobite Rebellion in her novel *The Bull Calves*.

Alice Munro: Oh, I should read that too, yes.

Chris Gittings: Getting back to your work, there are references to a repressive Scottish presbyterianism in for instance 'The Stone in the Field,' and *The Lives of Girls and Women*. And I'm just wondering what prompted you to cross the ocean and explore the history of the Covenanting armies that appears in 'Friend of My Youth' and 'Hold Me Fast, Don't Let Me Pass'?

Alice Munro: Well, I didn't really go there *exactly* to do that. It was the kind of thing that just sort of happened. The first time I went to Scotland was in 1982, I'd been to Norway on a book promotion thing and I thought I would just take a week and go to the Borders. And when I saw the country – I'd never even been to Edinburgh before – I loved it so much, I love the country and I love Edinburgh. And so I just wanted to come back and live there for a while. And because I did have this connection I could sort of make it respectable in a literary way, not that I was getting a grant or anything, but I could say well I'm doing something . . .

Chris Gittings: You could rationalize it . . .

Alice Munro: Yeah right! (laughter) Mainly, I just wanted to live there for a while. But it all did begin to interest me a lot, the whole history of the Covenanters.

Chris Gittings: Once you got there [Scotland] and you started getting into the history, did you see a connection with your own community back in Huron County?

Alice Munro: Oh yes, yes. I found out an interesting thing that I didn't know. You know I grew up in the United Church because that's what the Presbyterians had gone into here, but my background was fully Presbyterian, and I found that the Presbyterian Church in Canada doesn't arrive from the – maybe you know this – established Presbyterian church in Scotland.

Chris Gittings: No, I didn't realize that.

Alice Munro: It's a radical fundamentalist wing which came out here. There was something called the Glasgow Mission and they sent their own preachers out to Canada in say the 1840s, 1850s, and those preachers preached against the Presbyterian church as it was already established here because they figured it was not nasty enough I guess (laughter). And they founded Knox College in Toronto, and so what took over in Canada was really a kind of fundamentalist Presbyterianism, very narrow and tough.

Chris Gittings: Something that led to the strain of Cameronianism we see in 'Friend of My Youth.'

Alice Munro: Yes. So this isn't even the Presbyterianism of Scotland; it's a more difficult strain.

Chris Gittings: So once it is transposed to the Canadian context Presbyterianism becomes increasingly even more repressive?

Alice Munro: Well I think it did. I think that in the woods you know that in the hard life of the early settlers people often went crazy in one way and another, and many of them just went crazy with drink, and others maybe with philosophies like this because there was nothing for them to rub up against.

Chris Gittings: I guess religion can become some kind of substance abuse for some people.

Alice Munro: Yeah, yeah, it also may have kept them going of course. It gave an enormous drama, though a difficult one, to your life.

Chris Gittings: Did the two stories, 'Friend of My Youth' and 'Hold Me Fast, Don't Let Me Pass', develop independently of each other?

Alice Munro: Yes, yes. Someone told me the anecdote that 'Friend of My Youth' comes from, and it was just the bit about the two sisters and the Cameronians, and the man who was engaged to one of them getting the other one pregnant and their subsequent life. So I tried working that for a story, and then it began to work in with the story of my mother, and so that was the germ of the story. And the other one, ah, oh lord, I forget how it started.

Chris Gittings: I guess I'm thinking of a connection between those two stories in the form of that really violent and self-righteous Cameronianism that comes through at the end of 'Friend of My Youth' and in Hazel's reading up on Scottish history and the Covenanters.

Alice Munro: Yes, yes, but it isn't really what she finds there. She finds some other kind of repression in a way, a more ordinary kind I think.

Chris Gittings: Do you mean Dudley's situation with Antoinette and Judy?

Alice Munro: Yes, the two women that he's involved with and the suppressing of the one he probably really loves in the interests of respectability.

Chris Gittings: Yes, he has to work with the public.

Alice Munro: Yes, yes, I did get the feeling that would still be true there, but I'm not sure of that, are you?

Chris Gittings: This, I would take it from what I read, is a small village . . .

Alice Munro: Uuhm, it is actually Selkirk.

Chris Gittings: I think quite possibly. I know I have friends who are from further north, and they said you know that definitely in that area something like that would just not wash. I mean you shouldn't even read your newspaper on a Sunday in some of those communities.

Alice Munro: No, no, someone told me when I was there in '82, I wanted to go right up to the North and it turned out I was going to land in Wick on a Sunday.

Chris Gittings: (laughter) No, you don't want to do that.

Alice Munro: And they said 'Don't, don't, you won't even be able to get a cup of coffee.' (laughter)

Chris Gittings: It probably would have been an interesting experience though.

Alice Munro: Well, I'm rather comfort loving (laughter) so I didn't go.

Chris Gittings: You told me that you have been working on a project that concerns your own family history, and I was wondering if you could comment on your interest in family history as a writer?

Alice Munro: Well, I don't know what I could say – it's . . . I've found it's difficult because if you're used to writing fiction keeping oneself within the bounds of fact instead of taking that fictional germ and doing something with it is very difficult. So I still haven't hit on the form for the book – I keep coming closer to it all the time, and I have written a story which was in *The New Yorker* a while ago called 'A Wilderness Station,' have you seen it?

Chris Gittings: No, I haven't seen it yet.

Alice Munro: Well, it's the last story I had published, I forget when, but it was probably, oh some months back, probably in the spring. And it's actually about – it takes off from my ancestors coming up to Huron county, except that I have completely invented a dreadful macabre incident that takes place, and I have no justification for this at all.

Chris Gittings: It must be that Hogg blood in you coming out.

Alice Munro: (laughter) So you see, what may become of all this family history I'm not sure.

Chris Gittings: So you were thinking, initially, that you might like to do this as a non-fiction piece?

Alice Munro: Yes, yes, that's what I thought I should do, I thought it would be a pleasant change, but you're not always in control of what you can do. You sort of find out as you try to do it. So, I don't know how this will work out, but I have lots more material now, I have a lot of material.

Chris Gittings: When you're talking about this it reminds me a bit of Del Jordan, she says in *Lives of Girls and Women* 'It was not the individual names that were important, but the whole solid intricate structure of lives supporting us from the past' (26). Do you share that feeling?

Alice Munro: Oh yes, yes I think so. I think this is what people are in it for. And I guess I said in that piece that it doesn't really matter if any of these people – you know you see people hunting around for an ancestor just to know where the ancestor lived and died, just to know that there has been this whole support system, I guess that you are connected some how. . .

Chris Gittings: That there is some kind of continuity.

Alice Munro: Yes, and if you write fiction, you look for character, and I guess that's where I run into the difficulty because you get hints as to character, enough for a fiction writer, but not enough to make you justified to talk about this real person as if you knew what his character was. I've said his, and this is another problem. You know your male ancestors, at least I do, better than the females, and of course I've been following my father's family and what mainly happens is that mainly the letter-writers and the people about whom I know anything are men, except for James Hogg's mother.

Chris Gittings: Are there any women at all that stand out? Or do you only hear about them possibly through the men who are writing about them?

Alice Munro: Yes. I have one letter from my great great grandmother and it's a charming letter that she wrote to her future husband before they were married, and it's a letter in which she is trying to interest him in coming to see her, and evidently it worked.

Chris Gittings: And where were they living at this time?

Alice Munro: She was living in the Ettrick valley, and he had gone to work in the Highlands as a shepherd, you know that's when they were filling the Highlands with sheep?

Chris Gittings: Yes, with the cheviots.

Alice Munro: So that's why she was writing to him.

Chris Gittings: Have you touched on that as a possible story idea?

Alice Munro: Well, I've got it stored away, yes. And I've also got the fact that when the family came out to Canada they came – maybe I told you – in a sailing ship in 1818 – and they wrote letters home describing the voyage.

Chris Gittings: Do you have some of those?

Alice Munro: Yeah, and I have a fair bit of stuff.

Chris Gittings: How long have you been working away on this off and on?

Alice Munro: Well, it's kind of in the background, and it's an excuse for trips all over the country. I wouldn't say I'm working on it because I've been working on stories instead, but I think when I get the next book of stories together then I will take off on this other stuff, but who knows?

Chris Gittings: When do you think the next book of stories might be on its way to the press?

Alice Munro: No, I don't know – I've got about six stories done and I probably need eight or nine, so we'll see, but I'm not going to predict anything.

Chris Gittings: You remind me a bit of the narrator of 'Bardon Bus.' She is writing a family history that takes her to Australia.

Alice Munro: (laughter) That's right.

Chris Gittings: Does this kind of reflect what was going on at that time in the back of your mind?

Alice Munro: No, I don't think so. I think when I wrote that story I just wanted to have a reason for her going to Australia, and I knew people who did this and I know people who do ghost-writing so it seemed to me a plausible thing.

Chris Gittings: I meant to ask you earlier about the Scottish-Canadian writing of Ralph Connor and when you first encountered his work?

Alice Munro: Oh, well, Ralph Connor I saw as a Canadian writer, his Scottishness didn't really penetrate to me I guess. In the Sunday School library where I found most of my early reading, and of course they were full of Ralph Connor books.

Chris Gittings: And what did you think of Ralph Connor at that age?

Alice Munro: Listen, at that age I loved everything I read, and I seem to remember he's quite good with the wolves chasing the sleigh and things like that, it's quite exciting, isn't it?

Chris Gittings: That's right. I remember when I first started reading *The Man from Glengarry* I was being very pedantic and thinking, oh this is so sentimental, and then I got hooked, and I loved it, you know.

Alice Munro: (laughter) Yes, you know some of those writers were really good plotters, the writers whose point of view you disagree with. Oh, and another book I read because it was in the house, have you heard of a book called *Scottish Chiefs*?

Chris Gittings: No.

Alice Munro: It's by Jane Porter who was an early Victorian, I think Scottish, writer. This is about 1840 or so and the prose is very dense. It's very bad actually, it's a bad historical novel but what it is about is William Wallace. Do you know about William Wallace?

Chris Gittings: Yes.

Alice Munro: Good, and John Balliol, the puppet of the English and Robert the Bruce, and William Wallace was in there with his rebellion which I think got started in the Borders, and then another Scot betrayed him, which was not an infrequent event.

Chris Gittings: No (laughter).

Alice Munro: (laughter) They would be selling each other off.

Chris Gittings: Especially during the Clearances which came much later.

Alice Munro: Right. So I did read that. At that age I would read anything, I would just plough through a book like that, skipping a good deal I think, but getting the parts that were exciting.

Chris Gittings: You have said in other interviews that you often feel compelled to revise stories after publication. Are there any stories in *Friend of My Youth* that you would like to rework?

Alice Munro: Not yet, because I haven't looked at them. It's more apt to be earlier stuff that I would want to rework. I had to read one of my very first stories for some reason in Toronto a few years ago, and I just edited like mad as I went through it (laughter).

Chris Gittings: Will that editing appear in subsequent editions?

Alice Munro: No, no, I'm not at all sure that this is for the better; it's just that your writing changes, and it doesn't necessarily get better. You never know!

Chris Gittings: Oh, I think yours does.

Alice Munro: (laughter) Have you heard about Henry James who rewrote everything that seemed simple and clear when he wrote it and to make obscure and difficult in his old age? I think he did it for the academics.

Chris Gittings: Do you have a favourite story in *Friend of My Youth* or is it too recent?

Alice Munro: I never really have a favourite story, I have stories – I like the title story a lot. Generally stories that mean a lot to me personally I might say, but no not necessarily, but if I picked one it would probably be the title story.

Chris Gittings: That's a great story.

Alice Munro: Thank you.

Chris Gittings: The tension and ironic possibilities of the love triangle seem to hold a fascination for you as a writer and have been the subject of some truly wonderful stories. I'm thinking of 'Something I've Been Meaning to Tell You,' 'A Friend of My Youth', 'Hold Me Fast Don't Let Me Pass' and 'Wigtime'. What excites you about this type of material as a writer?

Alice Munro: Yes, I'm great on sisters too. Well, I'm not the first (laughter). I think if you go back maybe to Greece the love triangle was there. I think because it arouses such terrible emotions.

Chris Gittings: Do you think it allows the writer to explore parts of the psyche that otherwise might be obscured?

Alice Munro: Yes.

Chris Gittings: You mentioned that 'Friend of My Youth' might be one of your favourite stories if you were to pick one. The stricken mother figure who you have acknowledged is based on your own mother and her battle with Parkinson's disease haunts your work, I'm thinking of 'The Peace of Utrecht', 'Ottawa Valley' and most recently 'Friend of My Youth'. The narrator in 'Ottawa Valley' talks about the mother weighing her down and her failure to 'get rid of her'. Does 'Friend of My Youth' complete a process begun in 'Peace of Utrecht' of setting your mother free through your writing?

Alice Munro: I don't think so – it may. I notice that with personal material – I mean everybody's like this not just writers; the way you see your life does change as you grow older and so there is just a constant reworking of close personal material. I wouldn't say I was finished with that yet.

Chris Gittings: It seems like some kind of progress has been made since 'Peace of Utrecht' –

Alice Munro: Yes, yes it has.

Chris Gittings: Where in 'Peace of Utrecht' the narrator seems to all of the sudden realize that she is selling her mother short.

Alice Munro: Right.

Chris Gittings: And then at the end of 'Friend of My Youth', that wonderful line where the mother walks out of her prison, the image prison the daughter had constructed for her, it seemed she was kind of liberated in that way.

Alice Munro: I think what really has happened through those stories is that in a sense you become more and more dissatisfied with fiction, but of course you don't really or you wouldn't continue to write it. But the limitations of your own vision, I mean I think when you are about twenty you think you see your parents' life, lives, very clearly and generally very negatively, and then this changes as you grow older; you see things you didn't see before. Your whole judgement of that early landscape changes.

Chris Gittings: Well, I know with my own parents that you constantly hear little bits and pieces from other people that you didn't include in your construction of their characters, and it totally changes your vision of these people, they constantly shift in composition, it's interesting. That's one of the reasons I really enjoy that story.

Alice Munro: Oh, I know, that's right (laughter).

Chris Gittings: One of the things that fascinate me about 'Friend of My Youth' is the way the narrating daughter translates her mother's story of the Grieves family and Cameronianism into a narrative route toward her mother. Could you talk about this?

Alice Munro: Not really, I'm not good about talking about that sort of process because how I write it is all kind of a surprise to me. I don't mean it just suddenly flashes and it's there, but you know I was writing that story before I realized that it was my mother's story. You know I had the story of the sisters and out of this came the sort of story my mother would have made, and then out of this came *my* story of my mother. So I was sort of cocooning around something, around, and around and around. My mother did talk about being a writer I remember at one time and she talked a little bit about the kind of novel she would write, so I knew in a way.

Chris Gittings: That *The Maiden Lady* would be a reasonable facsimile of your mother's vision?

Alice Munro: Yes, yes, I was taking her point of view, the kind of fiction she would have made *as I saw it* when I was young, you know, which was with a certain amount of contempt.

Chris Gittings: And that comes across.

Alice Munro: Because her kind of fiction was not the kind of fiction that I considered important. I think I wanted to sort of explore that. So I think it's when I hit on this story as the story my mother would have told that it then became the story of my mother and me.

Chris Gittings: In a conversation with Elanor Watchell you talk about this process and comment that you ended up writing about writing a story. What does this type of writing allow you to do that a more conventional narrative might prohibit?

Alice Munro: Well, writing a story is just – it's not just writing I'm talking about really. I'm talking about the way people make stories. It's not just writers; everybody is making the story – at least many people make the story of their lives all the time and I think that's what interests me, and if I can sort of use the way one writes fiction to get at how we see our lives. I guess that's about all I can say about it.

Chris Gittings: Related to that – how people tell their stories and the materials they use – I'm thinking of 'Hold Me Fast, Don't Let Me Pass' and 'Friend of My Youth', it seems to me Hazel and the narrator of 'Friend of My Youth' are both trying to recover a piece of themselves through a transformative remembering of people in their pasts, and they do this, in part, through narratives of Scottish culture which seem to form some kind of connective tissue between them and their own personal stories. I find this very interesting.

Alice Munro: Oh I think people do this you know, I think it's interesting that you noted that because I hadn't really put it into words, but I think people use – well, a lot of people use music for instance. Well, you know the way people are about the Beatles, they are remembering whole chunks of their lives in a very strong and definite way. And people use poetry, they use stories. I could go through my life now from the age of about ten on just thinking about what I was reading, and the images and the different kinds of excitement, of the different sorts of reading you go through. This is something people don't generally write about, how big a part reading plays in your life, because it does, it's like a constant other room you go into besides the room you're living in.

Chris Gittings: Yes, it's interesting to see what people take out of that other room, but difficult to discern what they put into it. Speaking about reading, were you making a reference to the Scottish Kailyard in your description of the sentimental stories such as 'Wee MacGregor' that Flora force-fed to Ellie?

Alice Munro: Yes, I have that story in my house too, I remember 'Wee MacGregor'. 'Wee MacGregor' was an enormously popular sentimental novel of the Kailyard school, but only I didn't know then about the Kailyard school, do you?

Chris Gittings: I know a bit about it.

Alice Munro: That means cabbage yard, does it?

Chris Gittings: Yes, it does.

Alice Munro: They were homely stories of poor, good folk.

Chris Gittings: Yes, they were sentimental, idealized, and exaggerated portraits of rural Scottish life.

Alice Munro: I think Wee MacGregor was a rather bad boy, but he was a bad boy in a terribly acceptable way. He probably stole peppermints or something.

Chris Gittings: Would you classify what you constructed as your mother's novel, *The Maiden Lady*, as Kailyard?

Alice Munro: No, not quite, because they were highly concerned with being comic; they wanted to amuse people, but amuse them in a sentimental and respectable way. Hers would be much more the novel of sentimental power, it would be much more tragic.

Chris Gittings: What kind of a response did you get to 'Friend of My Youth' and 'Hold Me Fast, Don't Let Me Pass' in Scotland?

Alice Munro: Not much, not particularly, they were just interested that that was there. A review in one of the papers that I got since I've returned said that 'Hold Me Fast' was the only story that didn't capture an atmosphere because I didn't understand the Borders, but I thought that missed the point because actually I'm dealing with a Canadian woman's perception of the Borders. And I think that's very likely true because contemporary life there is not very open to me. After living there as long as you did, do you feel you know Scotland?

Chris Gittings: No, I lived there for two years, and I lived in Edinburgh. I got to know some Scots there, but Edinburgh is an entirely different world from Glasgow or the Borders. No, I don't think I have a good knowledge of the country. I wanted to talk a bit about 'Hold Me Fast, Don't Let Me Pass'. In discussing the Australian setting of 'Bardon Bus' with Geoff Hancock you said that you don't think setting matters all that much, that it's kind of incidental. How important is the Scottish setting in 'Hold Me Fast, Don't Let Me Pass'?

Alice Munro: Well, it's very important in what it evokes, and I think the Australian setting in 'Bardon Bus' is too, but the thing is I never set out to write about a place, only the place as it impinges on the characters, but it does have to be a certain sort of place, and it's probably more important in 'Hold Me Fast'.

Chris Gittings: Because for Hazel Scotland stimulates so many things within her, and she's hungry for that, and that's one of the reasons she goes there.

Alice Munro: Yes, but really what was interesting was her relationship with her husband, and something about the whole relationship between men and women in that age group.

Chris Gittings: I wanted to ask you about that. I loved the image of the shape-shifting man that appears in Margaret Dobie's recitation of the Scots ballad 'Tam Lin.' The ballad brought the whole story – its layers of narrative strands together for me; I saw Dudley and Jack as the shape shifting man and Antoinette, Hazel and Judy as Fair Jennets. How do you see the ballad working in the story?

Alice Munro: Yes, but I sort of didn't choose the ballad for that reason, but then I began to see that I had chosen it without realizing it because I know a lot of ballads and why did I choose that one? I chose it just because it always seemed to me so wonderful. And also you know Liz Lochhead has written a modern version of that ballad? And the content is, it's all very well when the man changes shape, but when the woman wakes up ugly what happens to her (laughter)? I think it's just a marvellous ballad and the setting is right there at Selkirk – for the ballad, Carterhaugh is a field just at the edge of Selkirk.

Chris Gittings: And there is this discrepancy about the location within the story.

Alice Munro: Yes.

Chris Gittings: I was wondering does Antoinette really believe it wasn't Carterhaugh? Or is she trying to tell Hazel something? Is this perhaps where Antoinette and Jack used to meet and the bells maybe prompted her to indicate this to Hazel, though covertly?

Alice Munro: Oh, I don't know, I don't think Antoinette is much given to memory, I think she is extremely practical.

Chris Gittings: Practical in the sense that she is selective?

Alice Munro: Selective, she remembers what is useful to her to remember. After all, she is lying about her age.

Chris Gittings: And her hair (laughter).

Alice Munro: And her hair, yes (laughter).

Chris Gittings: Could you comment on Hazel's apparent conflation of the Killing Times of Scottish history at Philiphaugh and World War Two and Jack? At the beginning of the story she writes 1945 in a journal entry concerning 1645 and Philiphaugh.

Alice Munro: Yes, well, I just thought that would be on her mind, but I don't think she is making a connection so much, she's just thinking of him being there in that room, and it's a very fortyish kind of room. You can imagine the soldiers being there with their girlfriends.

Chris Gittings: I loved that scene because all of the sudden her memories transport her back to Walley, Ontario.

Alice Munro: Yeah (laughter).

Chris Gittings: Are you familiar with Jack Hodgin's story 'The Lepers' Squint'?

Alice Munro: No, I'm not.

Chris Gittings: It's a story about a writer Desmond who goes back to his ancestral land of Ireland, and he's going to try and write a novel while he's there. In some ways Hazel's journey reminds me of Desmond's journey to Ireland – both find themselves in the role of tourist in a Celtic culture, and both investigate the history of that culture as part of their search for a story. Do you have any thoughts on the Canadian writer's return to the 'old country' – whether its Margaret Laurence and Scotland, Jack Hodgins and Ireland, Michael Ondaatje and Sri Lanka, or yourself and Scotland?

Alice Munro: Well, no, I don't really, I can't sort of see this from the outside. I know that to Australians this seems a kind of 'piss willy' thing to do, to go back, to think of yourself as having roots in Britain rather than thinking of yourself as belonging entirely to the new country.

Chris Gittings: And the Scots laugh as well.

Alice Munro: Yes, I know, so you become a kind of figure of fun.

Chris Gittings: But it seems important to people in this country to know – as you said earlier – what that structure is behind everything.

Alice Munro: Yes, I don't know, we never really repudiated what we call the 'old country' the way Americans did, and the way Australians to a later extent have. I mean, this may be a difficulty about forming a country, about our nationalism, I don't know. And especially I guess when I found the Hogg connection it was important for me. Because you would not have guessed in my family as I was growing up that there would be a poet, even though my father became a writer later on, all of this was so, so much buried beneath the importance of being a practical person and working hard in daily life. But it was all a great surprise to me.

Chris Gittings: I really appreciate your making the time to speak with me, it's been great. I've enjoyed it very much.

Alice Munro: So have I. 🖤

University of Birmingham

S. J. BOYD

'A Man's a Man': Reflections on Scottish Masculinity

'When there are so many we shall have to mourn . . .'

W. H. Auden

'Jock of Hazeldean' presents an image of Scottish manhood as we would like to 'see oorsels'. The 'ladie' in Scott's poem has the offer of being married to a very eligible young Englishman, the 'chief of Errington,/And lord of Langley-dale', no less. On the morning of their nuptials, however, she is discovered to be 'o'er the Border, and awa'/Wi' Jock of Hazeldean'.[1] Any Scotsman would interpret the *sententia* of this thus: Scotsmen are irresistible to women. Indeed, even a humble 'Jock' is preferable to a big-shot Englishman. The point is underlined if one sees the television recording of the Corries performing the song above the Tweed, Ronnie Brown looking every inch a Walt Disney version of a Border reiver. As so often in the nicely-polished glass of Scott's writings, it's a pleasing image of ourselves to contemplate. It's perhaps instructive to compare that image with the one which appears in the following little anecdote. The text here is not canonical, or even literary, but a conversation I overheard once between two girls on a bus in Dunfermline. They were speaking of their boyfriends. 'Does Alan hit you?' asked one. 'Naw, he disnae. Well, sometimes he hits me on the legs, like.' I thought this faintly sinister, but I was wholly unprepared for her friend's sad response: 'Derek hits me. [short pause] He hits me wi' a baseball bat.' I do not exaggerate when I say that even more appalling revelations followed. Hearing it all was an unpleasant experience, but a salutary one: when I am moved (and I *am* moved) by the ceremonials of Scottish arms and the glamour of the Scottish regiments, I remember the baseball bat of Dunfermline.

I hope that the gentle reader will excuse my use of anecdotal evidence. In this case at least it is reliable evidence, since I was myself the unwilling witness to it. Much of what follows will, however, be anecdotal, impressionistic, journalistic. A sociologist or criminologist might be able to correct some of the impressions I have: so much the better, but I am not a sociologist or criminologist. *Au contraire*, I'm a literary critic and I intend in this article to look at manifestations of or reflections on Scottish masculinity in literary texts, though I shall also draw on the text of my own life and experiences (as a Scotsman) for materials. I fear it will be impossible to avoid political incorrectness, for both nationalism and feminism seem to be PC in Scottish literary circles, but a survey of Scottish masculinity which simply *celebrated* its subject or suggested that it was the best kind of maleness on earth could only be regarded as a deliberate outrage upon feminist sensibilities. (Since I am neither a nationalist nor a feminist I am not particularly troubled by this double-bind, but I am aware of its existence.) For a sifting of the evidence tends to show that Scottish masculinity is a rather fiercely sexist beastie. Not for nothing is a book of interviews with Scottish and Irish women writers entitled *Sleeping with Monsters* (though there is, of course, a way to interpret that title which might accord with the Jock of Hazeldean version of the Scots male and his endowments). Still, consideration must also be given to the question of whether we are significantly worse than, or even different from, other nations in this regard, as also to whether shamelessly sexist attitudes have issued in any praiseworthy literary products.

SO MACHO?

It all begins with Tacitus. Before the inhabitants of North Britain had much chance to represent themselves in literature the Roman historian has Calgacus remind his warriors before Mons Graupius that they are the finest flower of manhood of the British Isles.[2] While there's every reason to suppose that Calgacus's famous speech was composed by Tacitus rather than recorded by him, it is not implausible to suppose that his father-in-law Agricola might have told him that the Caledonians did appear to have such attitudes. Almost two millenia later, Lewis Grassic Gibbon has a wry smile at the continuance of such views by having the folk-voice in *Sunset Song* refer to Calgacus as 'him that chased the Romans all to hell at the battle of Mons Graupius', a handily self-bolstering reversal of the actual result.[3] As a child at school in Dumbarton, I myself had a version of the Calgacus theory of Scottish manhood passed down to me by a teacher: the Roman Empire had stopped just outside Dumbarton because the Romans were frightened by the ferocity and prowess of the local warriors. Every boy in the class (and we were all boys) glowed with pride at that one, and no-one had the least difficulty in believing it was true. For Dumbartonians are 'Sons of the Rock', an entirely male people, hard as the basalt on which our ancient fortress stands. The manly rituals and warlike customs of the area in our own times have been keenly observed by Agnes Owens. Her

Mac informs us that he likes his facial scars: 'They were status for me.'[4] Mac's early adventures are recounted in a book entitled *Gentlemen of the West* (the title very properly ignoring the existence of female characters altogether) and the following is a representative sample of their (our?) *gentillesse*:

> Proctor's answer was to hurl a glass through the mirror behind the bar . . . My mother gave a moan of fear. This excited Paddy's chivalrous instincts. He hurried up to Proctor and smashed a lemonade bottle on the counter over his head.[5]

It perhaps bears saying that I was first attracted to Agnes Owens's work by the cover of the Penguin edition of *Gentlemen of the West*. The illustration, by Richard Adams, shows a brawl in a bar. One of the characters caught my eye as uncannily resembling a man I had known very well in Dumbarton. It was only much later I discovered that Agnes Owens lived in the Vale of Leven.

Drink and violence are, indeed, among the first words that spring to mind when one thinks on the notion of Scottish masculinity. That *may*, perhaps, be a little unfair to us, but it reflects how we are perceived by others and how we have presented ourselves to the world. In the realms of popular culture *Taggart* is a case in point, and the image of the Scots male I'm describing applies especially though not exclusively to Glasgow and 'the West' (Glaswegian has been described as the accent that grabs you by the lapels). At what is arguably a higher level of cultural production there is MacDiarmid's splendid essay on 'The Dour Drinkers of Glasgow', a snarling celebration of old-style Glaswegian pub-life, where men stood at the bar staring straight ahead to avoid provoking a fight by catching someone else's eye and to concentrate on the serious business of getting drunk:

> We feel no necessity whatever to indulge in any airs and graces, are not fond of promiscuous conversation . . . and if our risible faculties are moved at all by the human spectacle, that movement only adorns our faces intermittently with some sort of *risus sardonicus* . . . It is, indeed, a sort of fleeting facial comment hardly distinguishable from the effect of that gagging which an unwarily deep swig at what passes for whisky is apt to etch on the granitic features of even the most hardened soak.[6]

Unsurprisingly, since this is MacDiarmid, these qualities are contrasted with the characteristics of the English, who are (it is implied) a characteristically effeminate lot:

It is the old story of those who prefer hard-centre chocolates to soft, storm to sunshine, sour to sweet. True Scots always prefer the former of these opposites. That is one of our principal differences from the English. We do not like the confiding, the intimate, the ingratiating, the hail-fellow-well-met, but prefer the unapproachable, the hard-bitten, the recalcitrant, the malignant, the sarcastic, the saturnine, the cross-grained and the cankered, and the howling wilderness to the amenities of civilization, the irascible to the affable, the prickly to the smooth.[7]

To borrow a phrase from a pop-song, we are, quite simply, '*so* macho'. Our *machismo*, however, is of an odd kind. MacDiarmid's drinkers do not allow the presence of women in their pubs, though as a result of a decline in standards of maleness, as MacDiarmid makes clear in an aside of stunning sexism, this rule is being eroded: 'Men (if you can call them that) even take their wives and daughters along with them to these meretricious, deScotticised resorts.'[8] The Scotsman who enjoys female company in the hostelry is a Scots *man* no longer. It's a version of *machismo* which an Italian, or even an Englishman, might find hard to understand. Are MacDiarmid's Glaswegian hard men afraid of women?

Afraid of women they may be, but not apparently of anyone else. Their masculinity expresses itself better in acts of violence or war than in any kind of courtship ritual. MacDiarmid notes that the Scottish soldier has for centuries been 'famous as a bayonet-fighter' and adds that a 'similar preference for naked steel runs through every phase of our life'.[9] He is not alone among our major poets in emphasising our war-like propensities and qualities. Burns in 'The Vision' represents the men-folk of Kyle as Ossianic 'heroes . . . with feature stern', who 'brandish round the deepdyed steel/In sturdy blows;/While, back-recoiling, seem'd to reel/Their suthron foes'. The cowardly, unmanly English beat a hasty retreat when confronted by this 'martial race . . . /Bold, soldier-featur'd, undismay'd'.[10] Though this association of maleness with violence may be worrying or dismaying to a feminist, it is perhaps worthwhile to enter the plea that courage is an admirable virtue and that many, even among our 'suthron foes', would allow that there is truth in the assertions of MacDiarmid and Burns and that the Highland regiments have long been the *robur* of the British Army. 'Devils in Skirts', 'Ladies from Hell'; the German Army's hard-won compliments to the Highlanders confirm the validity of our claims of notable prowess on the field of battle while accusing them of transvestism, but the kilt, as Douglas Dunn points out in a recent sequence in which he adopts the point-of-view of the Scottish soldier down the years, is a garment well-adapted to the display of (frightening?) tokens of male power:

'Pour l'amour, oui; pour la guerre, non!'
Thus General Joffre – right *and* wrong.
Potatoes, chestnuts. – Hung like oxen,
Highland legends with posh frocks on.[11]

'Poison Dwarves' was a misleading description, or so legend would have it.

Such legends bolster the Scottish man's sense of his masculinity, *à la* 'Jock of Hazeldean'. It's extremely difficult to measure a nation's potency, and perhaps foolish even to speculate thereon, but a relevant section of Alexander Scott's somewhat Thersites-like poem 'Scotched' springs to mind as worthy of consideration:

> *Scotch Sex*
> In atween
> Drinks[12]

I fear that gets the order of priorities about right. One is reminded of the saying in Ireland, that *vetus et major Scotia*, that the quair fellow is someone who's more interested in women than drink. Trawling popular culture once more, one should not rule out the possibility that Rab C. Nesbitt, that grinning gargoyle, is a fit emblem of the alcoholico-sexual practices of many Scotsmen. (In one episode, incidentally, he *did* drunkenly look at and address a thistle.) If that is the case, it's little to be wondered at that a Scots*woman*, Liz Lochhead, should write of 'close-mouth kisses/which always/leave a lot to be desired'.[13] So much for the Jock of Hazeldean theory! Indeed, there are other poems by Lochhead, which I have written on elsewhere, which are more in keeping with the baseball bat of Dunfermline version of the matter.[14] In the most famous of all Scottish poems, 'Tam o' Shanter', sex is represented as something rather wicked, Satan's work, a desecration of the temple, accessed by drunkenness and enjoyed, even voyeuristically, at one's peril: Alexander Scott's summing up of '*Scotch Passion*' is 'Forgot/Mysel'.[15] Calvinism doubtless has much to answer for here, though it must be said that Roman Catholicism seems to produce similar results in the Hiberno-Caledonian world. The most spectacular voyeur and pervert in Scottish literature, Alasdair Gray's Jock McLeish, blames his twistedness in part on his moral father's consigning of sex to the realm of the devil:

> He would have detested the nasty sexual world I have devised.
> I am sure he felt in his bones that sexuality was wicked.
> Which is why I feel in my bones that wickedness is sexy.[16]

Man hands down misery to man. Our greatest poet, Byron, also a pervert and a strange, exotic growth of Calvinist culture, conveys the same sort of notion through epigrammatic deftness and outrageous *double entendre*:

> 'Tis pity, though, in this sublime world, that
>   Pleasure's a sin, and sometimes sin's a pleasure;
> Few mortals know what end they would be at . . . [17]

The Scotsman in love seems to have difficulty in expressing himself: terms of endearment do not come easily to him. Indeed, if Grassic Gibbon is a reliable authority, it would seem that mention of love at all is to be avoided, love being a word that belonged to 'the soppy English': 'you were shamed and a fool to say that in Scotland'.[18] Goodsir Smith's *persona* in 'New Hyne', a fine love poem, finds his 'craig' steik'd as he tries to express his tender feelings to his beloved.[19] Tom Leonard in 'A Summer's Day' superbly pits English eloquence in love, represented by the well-known Shakespeare sonnet alluded to in the title, against the expressive inarticulacy of his Glaswegian chatter-upper *persona*:[20]

> yir eyes ur
> eh
> a mean yir
> pirrit this wey
> ah a thingk yir
> byewtifl like ehm[21]

The *persona* here does manage to spit out 'ach a luvyi', but that little 'ach' does a lot to camouflage or qualify this embarrassing confession. Against this notion that the Scots are tongue-tied in love and poor at expressing tenderness there is the weighty evidence of Burns's love-songs, which it would not be unreasonable to describe as among the most famous and celebrated in the world. I feel, however, that regrettable though it may be, our national bard was more in tune with the spirit of his fellow-countrymen in a poem like 'Gie the lass her fairin':

> Syne coup her o'er amang the creels,
>   When ye hae taen your brandy,
> The mair she bangs the less she squeels;
>   An hey for houghmagandie . . .
>
> But coup her o'er amang the creels,
>   An bar the door wi baith your heels,
> The mair she *gets* the less she squeels;
>   An hey for houghmagandie.[22]

One doesn't have to be a feminist to feel that there's something rather objectionable in the sentiments expressed in this roistering little song.

The history of Scotland, in life and letters, is the history of a thorough-going patriarchy. Even in the sphere of religion it is noteworthy that Calvinism ditched the Blessed Virgin Mary (an unofficial female deity in the Catholic world and generally more popular than her more distinguished relations), leaving us with only a stern judgemental father-figure whose avatars are omnipresent in Scottish literature. Grassic Gibbon's John Guthrie springs to mind and, while it may be said that Gibbon is one of those writers who attempt to cut against the grain of Scottish patriarchy by 'boosting' the status of women, Chris being an assertive character and the very embodiment of Caledonia, still it must be replied that Chris is associated with the earth and men are the ones who drill and seed that earth. Similarly, MacDiarmid is concerned to praise and exalt the feminine principle, but writes poems in praise of whores and suggests that a woman's chief glory might be to pleasure some 'buck-navvy'.[23] Scottish patriarchy may not quite have succeeded in achieving the 'purest Monarchie' over women recommended by the very greatest of Scotsmen,[24] but until recent times it made a pretty good job of keeping women in their place (outside of pubs for example, and outside of the great public house of Scottish letters) and preventing their monstrous regiment.

SAME DIFFERENCE?

Douglas Dunn remarked to me, in a discussion of the strength of patriarchy in Scotland, that 'Mammy' is a mighty important personage in Scottish life. This is doubtless true, though tenderness in that direction can be difficult too, as *Gentlemen of the West* bears witness: ' "Goodnight," I said to her before I retired. I tried to add the word "mother" but since we seldom addressed each other by our names it was difficult.'[25] However, it is dubious whether 'Mammy' looms quite as large with us as does the mother-figure in Italian or Jewish communities, but it would be difficult to argue that Italian or Jewish culture was anything other than deeply patriarchal. Indeed, one might even suggest that the power of Mamma in the home often betokens female powerlessness anywhere else. However, such a cross-cultural comparison may serve usefully to remind us that it's a ticklish question to distinguish exactly what's *Scottish* about Scottish masculinity, what puts the *mac* in *machismo*, whether we're any worse (or better) than men in other cultures. *Machismo* is a Spanish word and it is to be doubted whether we Scots could equal traditional Hispanic culture in terms of institutionalised and everyday sexism. Even in the bar-room world (surprisingly) they may have the drop on us. It is, in my experience, a risky business to decline the offer of a drink in a Scottish pub, but when

Huxley's Anthony Beavis refuses a drink in Mexico, the affronted *hombre* answers this slight on his manhood by attempting to shoot him.[26] Few circumstances can be more conducive to displays of atavistic maleness than being in a football crowd, but it's abundantly clear that the supposedly effeminate English have in recent years utterly outstripped us in manifestations of football-fan yobbishness. Indeed, Scots fans have become so well-behaved as to be popular the world over and irresistible to Swedish policewomen. There are baseball bats in cupboards south of the border too and we have little to be ashamed of in a comparison with our nearest neighbours.

In the realm of letters, however, manifestations of *machismo* loom rather large, more so, I think (though such generalizations are obviously risky), than in the literature of our nearest neighbours. A prominent figure in the literature of our neighbours, the *arbiter elegantiae* Matthew Arnold, makes some infamously un-neighbourly comments about our national bard and our enthusiasm for him. For Arnold, Burns and his countrymen are rather too concerned with 'Scotch drink, Scotch religion, and Scotch manners', this is 'a harsh, a sordid, a repulsive world' and Burns's perpetual involvement with it debars him from entry to Arnold's Premier League of great poets.[27] Arnold's somewhat patronising attitude has not won him many friends among Scots *literati*, but one should, in fairness, recognise that he is, rather reluctantly, excluding Burns from a pantheon made up of the Homers, Dantes, Shakespeares and Miltons of this world: Burns is praised with faint damn. There is also, leaving aside the value judgement, some substance to Arnold's claim with regard to Scottish literature in general and this has relevance to the subject of this essay. Of 'Scotch manners' one might note that a tiny incident in *Sunset Song* shows that they can be more blatantly masculinist than English manners: 'Syne Chae had the toddy made and he handed a glass to Ewan first, as was right with a man, and another to Chris.'[28] The aspect of Arnold's censure which is of greatest relevance here however is, of course, the matter of 'Scotch drink'.

'Leeze me on drink!'[29] Burns is not alone among our literary men in making much of an enthusiasm for John Barleycorn. Indeed, Scottish writers seem to be hard drinkers *ex officio*. Jock McLeish recalls from his experience of the Edinburgh Festival this scene in a pub in Hanover Street:

> The bar was crowded except where three men stood in a small open space created by the attention of the other customers. One had a sombre pouchy face and upstanding hair which seemed too like thistledown to be natural, one looked like a tall sarcastic lizard, one like a small sly shy bear. 'Our three best since Burns,' a bystander informed me, 'barring Sorley of course.'[30]

Young Jock does not recognise MacDiarmid, MacCaig and Garioch and might be forgiven for thinking that the bystander was pointing out Scotland's three finest drinkers (apart from the 'barred' Sorley!). The customers make space for their poets, to attend on their every word *and/or* to watch the bards at their junketings. As Buck Mulligan remarks, 'the bards must drink and junket',[31] and Scotch bards must drink and junket *gu leòr*. There are countless anecdotes along the lines of 'went round to interview X (bard and shennachie)/drinking Laphroaig/woke up three days later' and the fact that they are perhaps mostly untrue is really neither here nor there. We feel they *ought* to be true. It's for this reason, doubtless, that Sydney Goodsir Smith, who as bard-and-boozer par excellence would have felt disappointed at being left out of Gray's poets' pub scene, descends occasionally to faintly MacGonagallesque proclamations of his fondness for a quiet dram (or twenty):

> And sae we come by a route maist devious
> Til the far-famed Aist-West Synthesis!
> Beluved by Hugh that's beluved by me
> And the baith o' us loe the barley-bree –
> But wha can afford to drink the stuff?[32]

Here Goodsir Smith, who once gave his hobbies as 'drinking and blethering',[33] seems to allow drunken blethers to break in, with bar-room irrelevance, to his verse. He can also evoke with some *bravura* however, as here in *The Vision of the Prodigal Son*, the sheer exhilaration of the Scottish pub, that offers escape from the constraints of the workaday world and where drink can transform, in true Dionysian fashion, even what's dirty and malodorous in the human world to something attractive:

> I was standan at the bar, a gless in my nieve,
> Fleean wi the insolence of Friday nicht –
> A rabble o' cronies, lauchter,
> Blethers, din, the clink of gless,
> The reik, the stour, the stink,
> The blissit libertie of booze in action . . . [34]

Perhaps it's a desire to be one of the gang that prompts Garioch to publish a sonnet about how the Scots' 'True Rhymer' (he himself) was caught urinating in the street by a policewoman (not Swedish, alas).[35] A similar spirit of far-from-contrite confessionalism is found in Tom Leonard's witty 'Non Sum Qualis Eram Bonae Sub Regno Cynarae', where the English poet Edward Dowson's phrase 'between the kisses/and the wine . . . I have been faithful to thee' is spectacularly expanded to include 'wee heavies . . . whyte and mackay's' etc, etc, eleven forms of booze in all, and three prohibited substances for good measure![36]

MacDiarmid places himself very pointedly *among* the dour drinkers of Glasgow, men with granitic features, hard men: 'Hail Caledonia, stern and wild!' He is not above threatening the reader:

> Scots of that particular mettle are the very salt of the earth. I am one of them and so I know. It would not pay anyone to dispute the point in any of the Glasgow pubs I frequent.[37]

Wha daur meddle wi' Chris Grieve (and pals)? MacDiarmid's 'Theory of Scots Letters' rests on some fairly masculinist foundations: the vernacular, for example, 'keeps alive a spirit of brave and virile gaeity'.[38] His post-vernacular poetry-of-hard-fact might even be interpreted as attempting to create an *écriture masculine*, the stony limits of male discourse. A certain re-joicing in hardness, whether one's own or that of one's fellow Scots (-men) is not uncommon. Garioch's sonnet 'I'm Neutral', which describes how he was accosted in the street by some thuggish gang-member, ends with the casual 'Aweill, I caa'd him owre, and that was that'.[39] *Nemo poetas nostros impune lacessit.* Glaswegian hardness (world-famous, though one wonders how long Glasgow's finest would last in Detroit or Philadelphia) certainly provides eye-catching decor in the poetry of Edwin Morgan and Tom Leonard. Morgan's 'Glasgow Sonnets' begins thus: 'A mean wind wanders through the backcourt trash. Hackles on puddles rise . . .'.[40] In Mean City even the puddles seem to be squaring up for a barney. Leonard is capable of poking fun at the *machismo* of Glaswegians: 'The Hardmen' suggests that the butch bluster may be a cover for homosexual inclinations.[41] But Leonard is a very determined 'bunnit hussler' and his poetry offers powerful representations of male violence, in 'No Light' for example,[42] and he can be even more threatening than MacDiarmid. In 'Good Style' he addresses those readers who find his Glaswegian impenetrable (and an affront, presumably, to notions of good style):

> jiss try enny a yir fly patir wi me
> stick thi bootnyi good style
> so ah wull[43]

How's that for Nesbitt-ism? The Glasgwegian poet has his own version of good style: it involves putting the boot in – with a flourish. In 'Pffff' Leonard's *persona* gives a wonderfully convincing account of being solicited by a teenage prostitute:

middla Sucky Hall Street
fuckin big hard dawn
nearly shot ma load[44]

The physiological blends into the meteorological to create a stunning urban landscape, Sunrise over the Taggart Country.

THE PROOF OF THE [BLACK] PUDDING

Scottish masculinity, then, even as it manifests itself among our poets, is not something that anyone of a PC disposition can easily approve of. Objectionable attitudes, however, are no bar to literary excellence, obvious examples being *Paradise Lost* and *The Faerie Queene*. Within the Scottish tradition and the context of masculinity, one might point to 'Tam o' Shanter' and *A Drunk Man Looks at the Thistle* as cases in point. I want to look closely at a smaller-scale and less well-known example, however. It is 'The Black Bull o' Norroway' by Sydney Goodsir Smith,[45] the frontispiece to whose *Collected Poems* shows him hard at the bardic business in an Edinburgh pub. Goodsir Smith was, indeed, perhaps the champion drinker of all Scottish poets (in a journal called *Scotlands* the fact that he was a New Zealander need not trouble us overmuch). The poem is at the epicentre of his sequence of love poems *Under the Eldon Tree*, where it forms a pendant with the other central poem 'Orpheus'. Both describe descents into the underworld; in the case of 'Orpheus' a rather dignified, classical Hades, in the case of 'The Black Bull' a grotesque contemporary world of low-life found 'Down the stair' (4) in Leith Street, Edinburgh.

A bare synopsis of the poem shows that it is a testament of spectacular debauch. The poet, after 'Sevin nichts and sevin days' (30) of bevvying, falls in with a sixteen-year-old prostitute ('Her mither in attendance'!) (97). They spend 'a nicht o' lust' (183) together, during which, the poet remembers with '*belle nostalgie de la boue*', she 'cack't the bed in exstasie!' (181). It is not a model of political correctness. In this context one might note that the title itself could be taken as an allusion to Hogg's *Confessions of a Justified Sinner*, for important events in that novel take place in an Edinburgh howff of that name, though it seems to have moved between the times of Robert Wringhim and Sydney Goodsir Smith.[46] The intertextual link prompts one to ask: how is Goodsir Smith's sinful behaviour justified. By his being a poet? By his being a Scotsman (or New Zealander!)? By his being a Scottish poet?

The 'sins' of the Scots poet are much in evidence in the poem. There is a deal of 'braggandie' about feats of drinking, as here, where Goodsir Smith complains that the barman spoke to him in a manner not appropriate to his status as 'Bard and Shennachie' and Master of Arts:

- The whilk rank and statioun I haud
In consequence and by vertue
O' unremittan and pertinacious
Applicatioun til the bottle
Ower a period no exceedan
Fowr year and sax munce or moneths
(The latter being a *hiatus* or *caesura*
For the purposes o' rusticatioun
Or *villeggiatura*
   'At my place in the country')
                                                    (69–78)

The aureate diction (or is it dictioun?) serves only to emphasize the MacGonagallesque quality of the lines, blethering out a plethora of facts that we didn't really need to know or wish to be told. In fairness to MacGonagall one should perhaps say that it would be still more appropriate to describe this stylistic excess as MacDiarmidian (or perhaps Grievous). Goodsir Smith carries such Dutch-realist literal mindedness to staggering extremes here:

Her shanks were lang, but no owre lang, and plump,
   A lassie's shanks,
Wi the meisurance o' Venus –
   Achteen inch the hoch frae heuchle-bane til knap,
   Achteen inch the cauf frae knap til cuit
As is the true perfectioun calculate
By the Auntients after due regaird
For this and that,
      The true meisurance
   O' the Venus dei Medici,
   The Aphrodite Anadyomene
And aa the goddesses o hie antiquitie –
   Siclike were the shanks and hochs
O' Sandra the cou o' the auld Black Bull.
                                                    (102–15)

These lines have an oddly Scottish quality of being both dreadful and superb at the same time. Typically for this poem, they impact grotesque Scottishness upon classical beauty, a pattern, as observed above, identifiable in the poem's juxtaposition with 'Orpheus' in the sequence and, one might add, in Edinburgh topography: from the Playfair Library to the Grassmarket is but a step. It's hard to believe that the goddess Aphrodite could possess in her person anything so outlandish as a 'heuchle-bane', but in this Scots 'translation' she does. The grinning gargoyle deals out 'true meisurance' to the goddesses of antiquity *and* to Sandra. It is Goodsir Smith at his most worthily Joycean: the classical pantheon is dragged 'doun the stair' and the contemporary whore is granted an apotheosis. The 'bardic ee', in a most deft reference to the [tongue-tied Saxon] Bard, are 'In a fine frenzie rollan' (25–6), but the Scots bard's eyes are rolling because he is 'Fou as a puggie' (of course!). He glances from earth (Sandra) to heaven (Venus) and the net effect is to confuse the two. Indeed, the lunatic-lover and poet of 'The Black Bull' mixes both heaven and hell, making a beast of himself yet winning one night with a veritable Queen of the Faeries under the Dionysian power of drink: his apostrophe to Sandra, 'My Helen douce as aipple-jack/That cack't the bed in extasie!', is a marriage of heaven and hell of which, we may be certain, Joyce would have approved.

The approval of Joyce, who is, at least *prima facie*, a double-dyed male chauvinist, is unlikely to work effectively as an *argumentum de auctoritate* with many feminists. Goodsir Smith's *persona* in the poem certainly displays some typically sexist Scottish attitudes, though it is possible that these are subject to irony. Sandra is a 'cou' (42, 95), available for the convenience of any old bulls. The poem opens with the somewhat brutal expression 'I got her' and, although Sandra is honoured with a Petrarchan coronation of 'bays,/Laurel and rosemarie and rue' (188–9), it is dangerously two-faced about members of her profession. The 'hures o Reekie' are 'bonnie *craturies*' (23) but also 'Dour as stane, the like stane/As biggit the unconquerable citie/Whar they pullulate,/Infestan/The wynds and closes' (17–21). The whores are at once attractive and a disease, an infestation. 'Pullulate' derives, as a good classicist like Goodsir Smith would have known, from a Latin word meaning 'the young of any creature', an etymological nicety of some point given the tender age of Sandra the cou (or calf).

The *persona*'s attitudes and behaviour do not redound to his credit, but they are manifested in (and perhaps productive of) poetry of high quality. The vision of respectable Edinburgh transformed to a 'thrang mercat' (133) of copulation 'I' the buts and bens/ And single ends,/The banks and braes/O' the toueran cliffs o' lands' (137–40) is remarkable. Edinburgh topography (of the Old Town) lends itself to the atavistic shift from civilization to the barbaric or outlandish, from culture back to nature. The intertextual glance at a sentimental Burns love-song gives a neat twist, especially as the *persona* will end the poem by speculating that Sandra may have given him 'the pox', a particularly painful thorn to be left with. The picture of Sandra *post coitum* is both sad and magnificent:

There Sandra sleepan, like a doe shot
I' the midnicht wuid . . .
Her flung straucht limbs
A paradisal archipelagie
Inhaudan divers bays, lagoons,
Great carses, strands and sounds,
Islands and straits, peninsulies,
   Whar traders, navigators,
   Odyssean gangrels, gubernators,
   Mutineeers and maister-marineers
And aa sic outland chiels micht utilise wi ease
Chaep flouered claiths and beads,
Gauds, wire and sheenan nails
   And siclike flichtmafletherie
In fair and just excambion
For aa the ferlies o' the southren seas
That chirm in thy deep-dernit creeks . . .
                 (161–79)

Quotation *in extenso* is necessary to convey the full (highly complex) effect.
There is the brutal forthrightness of the suggestion that the wonders of
the south seas gurgle in the deep dark creeks of Sandra's body, but this is
held in tension with the tender image of her as the wounded doe, an image
which appeals to a courtly world of hart-hunting and yet suggests that *this* is
where all such courtliness leads and which is further complicated by one's
awareness that it is the speaker who has done the shooting. (Who killed
Bambi?) There is also the Donne-like expansion of the woman's body into
an earthly paradise, an India, a mine of precious stones, making the little
room an everywhere.[47] The superb variation on this Donne strategy lies in
Sandra's being compared to virgin territory or a primitive culture that can
easily be colonised by men. Virgin territory is perhaps a misleading expression in this context, since the persona is aware that Sandra's paradisial body
can be, and *probably has been*, bought for buttons by any old dirty *matelot*; a
sobering thought. A profound pity for the girl is detectable here, especially
as the *persona* has earlier observed that 'Her een were, naiturallie, expres-
sionless,/Blank as chuckie-stanes, like the bits/O' blue-green gless ye find
by the sea' (116–18). Perhaps this is Sandra's defense-mechanism against
the horrors of her life of exploitation; perhaps it shows that she has come
to value herself at her own price (or is it her mother who sets the tariff?).
At any rate, it does not prevent our bard from putting down his money
and joining the crew of gangrels. Indeed, though there is mention of 'sweet
regrets' (119), the *persona*, for all his tender pity and Iago-like awareness

of the realities of the prostitute's life,[48] seems to adopt what is very largely an attitude of *'moi, je ne regrette rien'* to the shocking confessions of the poem, the final line being a shoulder-shrugging 'Ach, weill!' It is a phrase which exactly sums up my own attitude to Scottish masculinity and to the opprobrium which I fear this little squib will bring upon me. ♥

University of St Andrews

1   Sir Walter Scott, 'Jock of Hazeldean', ll. 11–12, 31–32.
2   Tacitus, *Agricola*, 30–32. Testimony to the fierceness, courage and prowess in battle of the Celts is found in a number of authors of classical antiquity, including Aristotle, Strabo, Polybius, Diodorus Siculus and Ammianus Marcellinus.
3   L. G. Gibbon, *Sunset Song*, Heritage of Literature Series (Harlow, Essex: Longman, 1971), p. 18.
4   Agnes Owens, *Gentlemen of the West* (Harmondsworth: Penguin, 1986), p. 61.
5   Agnes Owens, p. 49.
6   Hugh MacDiarmid, 'The Dour Drinkers of Glasgow' in *The Thistle Rises*, edited by Alan Bold (London: Hamish Hamilton, 1984), pp. 212–13.
7   Agnes Owens, pp. 210–11.
8   Agnes Owens, p. 208.
9   Agnes Owens, p. 211.
10   Robert Burns, 'The Vision', ll. 93–102, 111–13.
11   Douglas Dunn, *Dante's Drum-Kit* (London: Faber and Faber, 1993), p. 132 ('Dressed to Kill', III).
12   Alexander Scott, *Selected Poems 1943–1974* (Preston: Akros Publications, 1975), p. 62.
13   Liz Lochhead, *Dreaming Frankenstein & Collected Poems* (Edinburgh: Polygon, 1984), p. 151 ('Cloakroom').
14   See S. J. Boyd, 'The Voice of Revelation: Liz Lochhead and Monsters' in *Liz Lochhead's Voices*, edited by Robert Crawford and Anne Varty (Edinburgh: Edinburgh University Press, 1993), pp. 38–56
15   Alexander Scott, *Selected Poems*, p. 62 ('Scotched').
16   Alasdair Gray, *1982, Janine* (Harmondsworth: Penguin, 1985), p. 157.
17   Byron, *Don Juan*, Canto the First, CXXXIII.
18   *Sunset Song*, p. 128.
19   Sydney Goodsir Smith, *Collected Poems 1941–1975* (London: John Calder, 1975), p. 158.
20   There is a certain irony in this. It has been remarked that the further north and east one goes in Scotland, the less speech is approved of. George Mackay Brown is proud of the extreme taciturnity of his fellow Orcadians. Seen from Peterhead, Glasgow is a city of dreadful eloquence.
21   Tom Leonard, *Intimate Voices* (Newcastle upon Tyne: Galloping Dog, 1984), p. 41. As is often the case with Leonard, lively verbal games are going on beneath the surface of the *patois*. Given the amatory context, there's a glorious ambiguity about the phrase 'pirrit

this wey', and he who speculates on how the woman addressed might be beautiful like M will not go unrewarded.

22   Burns, 'Gie the lass her fairin', ll. 5–8, 13–16.
23   MacDiarmid, 'In the Slums of Glasgow' (1935), ll. 68–77.
24   James Graham, Marquis of Montrose, 'An Excellent New Ballad', l. 4.
25   Owens, pp. 46–7.
26   Aldous Huxley, *Eyeless in Gaza*, ch. XLI.
27   See Arnold's 'The Study of Poetry'.
28   *Sunset Song*, p. 134.
29   Burns, 'The Holy Fair', st. 19.
30   Gray, p. 282.
31   James Joyce, *Ulysses*, Corrected Text; edited by Hans Walter Gabler with Wolfhard Steppe and Claus Melchior (Harmondsworth: Penguin, 1986), p. 13.
32   Smith, *Collected Poems*, p. 155 ('Slugabed', ll. 40–44).
33   Smith, p. xii.
34   Smith, p. 192.
35   Robert Garioch, *Complete Poetical Works*, edited by Robin Fulton (Edinburgh: Macdonald Publishers, 1983), p. 91 ('A Fair Cop').
36   *Intimate Voices*, p. 128.
37   *The Thistle Rises*, p. 214.
38   *The Thistle Rises*, p. 132.
39   Garioch, p. 82.
40   Edwin Morgan, *Selected Poems* (Manchester: Carcanet, 1985), p. 78.
41   Leonard, p. 58.
42   Leonard, p. 59.
43   Leonard, p. 14.
44   Leonard, p. 56.
45   Smith, *Collected Poems*, pp. 167–71. Line-references to this poem are given in brackets in the text.
46   It seems to have moved again since. Last time I looked, it was in the Grassmarket.
47   See Donne's 'The Good Morrow', 'The Sun Rising', 'Love's Progress' and 'To his Mistress Going to Bed'.
48   See *Othello*, IV. i. 94–5.

An Interview with Helena Kennedy

Helena Kennedy was born in Glasgow in 1950, leaving the city when she was seventeen to study in London for the Bar. She is a QC practising mainly in criminal law, and has acted in many important cases including the Guildford Four appeal. She is the Vice-President of the Haldane Society of Socialist Lawyers and Chair of Charter 88, and writes and broadcasts on issues connected with the law, civil liberties and women. Her book, *Eve Was Framed*, which investigates the ways in which British justice discriminates on the grounds of sex, was published in 1992 by Chatto & Windus. The interview took place in London in January 1994.

Jean McNicol: I'd like to start by talking about your upbringing in Glasgow.

Helena Kennedy: I'm a Southsider, and now when I go back I have great problems finding my way around the north of the city: you never went out of your own patch. So I was brought up on the Southside and my parents were Southsiders. We first lived in a tenement just at the end of Allison Street where it joins Nithsdale Street and I lived there until I was ten and then my parents got a council house in Pollokshaws. My father was what was called a 'bundle-strangler' down here in slang: he was a dispatch hand for the newspapers so he was really on constant night shift. The newspapers would come off the press and the men would tie them up and get them into the vans to be on your doorstep in the morning. That's what he did most of the time when I was growing up. When we were little, when he came back from the war, he managed a pub for a while, but he wanted to get into the newspapers and was unemployed for a while and was a casual worker until he was eventually taken on.

Jean McNicol: You've talked before about your father being a socialist and involved in his union.

Helena Kennedy: He was always a socialist and when he worked in newspapers he was very involved with his union. Both he and my mother were very socialist. A lot of it, of course, came out of the fact that the majority of people in Glasgow are anyway.

Jean McNicol: Do you feel that the socialist and ILP background which many people in Glasgow had meant that there was more emphasis on and acceptance of women and working-class people in general being educated and going to university than there was in the general population at the time?

Helena Kennedy: One of the things that I think's quite interesting about Scotland is that although I was brought up in a Catholic family in Glasgow, there's absolutely no doubt that Presbyterianism is one of the important cultural elements that makes Scotland as socialist as it is. There's much less tugging of the forelock and there's much more acceptance of equality and the ideal of it, and I think that permeated all our lives – even those who were not part of the Presbyterian tradition. It certainly was part of our culture. That tradition was so deep-rooted in Scotland that it was part and parcel of the Labour tradition and it meant that Scotland, happily, did not go down the same route of horrible sectarian division that happened in Northern Ireland. I think that the Labour Party welded together the socialism of Catholics and Protestants.

Jean McNicol: Do you think that there's still a different, more cohesive political culture in Scotland, or is it different from England only in that the Labour Party is the Establishment in Scotland?

Helena Kennedy: There are elements of that which can be disheartening, that it's just a different kind of Establishment.

Jean McNicol: Do you think it's true that Scots have a very strong sense of their national identity, which is strongly linked with their political and social culture, but that this clear sense of identity is something people in England don't really share and that this has a great deal to do with the problems Britain faces at the moment?

Helena Kennedy: I agree with that. I think they've got a lot to do with the question of identity and I think it's also one of the problems that gives rise to a much lesser social cohesion down here. It's one of the reasons why I suppose I've felt an increasing urgency to be back with my ain folk and spend more time in Scotland.

Jean McNicol: You came down here to study when you were quite young, seventeen. I did the same thing, but I didn't think then what the ramifications were, that it would be that much harder to go back.

Helena Kennedy: I think it may be that women are more like that than men. I've never planned anything in my life, I didn't come down with some great career plan, it sort of happened. At no time did I have a life plan, it's just that this is where the road has taken me, but the nice thing now is that I spend much more time in Scotland with my sisters and their children, which is great.

Jean McNicol: Why do you think you did leave?

Helena Kennedy: It was about reading books and thinking that you had to travel and see other places in order to widen your horizons. I was quite hungry to see what life was like elsewhere. The ghastly thing now is that because of the economics of higher education those privileges of going away are going to be the privileges of a small minority. Adversity can create challenges for you that you can either decide to take up or not, and coming away meant that I had to make a success of it, I couldn't admit to not liking things.

Jean McNicol: I think it's one of those Scottish traits that it's very hard to go back with your tail between your legs.

Helena Kennedy: That's right, exactly. You have to make it, you have to do it, you have to succeed at it, and so I think that maybe life would have been entirely different had I stayed in Scotland. There's no way you can start re-examining the past, I just think that I was presented with many more challenges than I might have had otherwise and in that bloody-minded way that we Scots have I just felt required to do the best at it.

Jean McNicol: How do you feel about the possibilities of devolution and independence for Scotland and do you believe in the much-touted cultural renaissance?

Helena Kennedy: I think there are far more exciting, interesting things happening in Scotland than elsewhere. I think it's a much more invigorating environment and the question to ask is why should that be? I think it's partly because people aren't feeling totally downtrodden and cowed, although they're feeling angry there's a way of giving expression to that.

Jean McNicol: Devolution would bring with it the necessity of a Scotland Act, and thus some element of a written constitution. Could the question of Scotland be a catalyst for more general constitutional change?

Helena Kennedy: I think it actually has been already: a lot of the energy for constitutional change has come out of Scotland. Some of my own commitment to this has come from working with American lawyers. I've spent some time in the United States and have close connections with civil rights lawyers who've been involved in working with the American constitution. What happened to us here in Britain was that in the early Seventies we took on some of those things that came via North America, ideas about equal opportunities legislation or race relations legislation. But we didn't have a rights tradition, an intellectual tradition within the law, or even on the Left, that was about rights. At first I was resistant to the idea of having a Bill of Rights at all because I thought that giving power to judges was a bad thing – a shared view among the Left – but now I've come to feel that we can't just bury our heads and say that judges are as they always were and always will be, you have to do something about the nature of our judiciary.

Jean McNicol: A lot of figures on the Left have resisted this. Stephen Sedley, who was recently made a High Court judge himself, said constitutional reform was not a cause for a true radical and 'would blow up in everybody's faces because it gave too much power to judges'. What kind of changes to the appointment and practices of the judiciary do you favour? You've just talked about the American system, but the Supreme Court there has many failings, for example, the recent upholding of the death penalty for minors and the mentally defective.

Helena Kennedy: Stephen said that before he became a High Court judge and perhaps he'll take a different view now. I don't think that you've given a very fair description of the US Supreme Court. It is, like courts everywhere, fairly reactionary but there's no doubt that it was very important in changing American society. Of course, courts don't change things, but they can put the stamp of authority on change and the changes that came through the civil rights movement were ultimately endorsed for a wider public by the Supreme Court. Like it or not we are moving in a certain direction in Britain where there will inevitably be more and more decisions made by courts in Europe, so we have to engage with the question of what we are going to do about all this. I would advocate changes in how our judges are appointed and how they are trained, how they're kept on their toes, even if we weren't talking about a Bill of Rights, but I think a Bill of Rights is actually about something that's happening in the wider world, about the commitment to human rights becoming the big idea of the late twentieth century, in the way that democratic rights, the right to vote, were the great ideas at the end of the nineteenth century. We're going down that road anyway so we'd better get our act together and start thinking through the implications of it and make sure that we get the kind of Bill of Rights that progressive people would like to see. To go back to where we started, I think Scotland has been important, because hearing that voice has been very important for me and putting it together with other feelings I've been carrying about as a lawyer has to mean quite a big shift constitutionally. One of the reasons why I've decided to put my energies into chairing Charter 88 since the last election is that I really do think that we've got to look again at what's happening.

There are no new ideas around, not only is this Government bereft of ideas – the Right had one idea and that was Monetarism and we've seen the failure of that – the problem is that the Left too has no ideas and that's why we're hearing nothing from the Opposition. I think you have to shift the furniture, the constitutional architecture, in order to generate new ideas and that's why I think that this is the crucial activity that people should be involved in.

Jean McNicol: On the subject of the connection between change in Scotland and Britain as a whole, there is a view that the problematic link between English national identity and the Ukanian nation-state means that any political reform based on that political nation is bound to fail.

Helena Kennedy: The thing that gets you away from that is Europe, I don't think we can get away from what the implications of our relationship with Europe are, they are considerable, and I don't think people have really taken that on board yet.

Jean McNicol: Britain holds the record number of cases decided against any country by the European Court of Human Rights, which does make one rather sceptical about handing judges even more power. Obviously you would favour changing the ground rules, but you can't just sack the existing judiciary overnight.

Helena Kennedy: This Government, desperately looking around for new ideas when it's decided that family values have not been such a good idea, will decide that they should not allow foreign judges to make decisions and they will incorporate the European Convention on Human Rights into British law with no reform of the judiciary to go with it. Then we really will have the problems that we're talking about, with the judiciary having that power with none of the things that we would see as being necessary, such as proper accountable procedures for appointing judges and a backdrop of principle which they can work against. I feel that we are deciding rights without any of those other things being in place.

Jean McNicol: Do you think that constitutional change would make people feel that they had more of a stake in their country, that they were citizens rather than subjects?

Helena Kennedy: I am not deluded enough to imagine that creating constitutional change in itself is going to be the panacea for all ills but I do think that something ghastly is happening whereby more and more people are feeling completely and utterly uninterested in politics, they feel disenchanted, they think all politicians aren't worth a candle and this is one reason why there is a dearth of talent among those choosing a political career: very few talented, bright young people choose to go into it. From time to time people ask me why I don't think of doing it, and then I think, 'doesn't one have a clearer voice not being involved in all of that and being able to speak one's heart without having to follow the party line?' I think that could be rather hard, the business of having to pretend that you agree with your colleagues when they're talking nonsense. So I really do think people are very disenchanted and so if talking about what we want out of a Bill of Rights, what we want out of Parliament, what we want if we are to have real subsidiarity where the decisions are made closer to the ground, if that creates more discussion and more political discourse then that has to be a good thing. I think it has to be one of the things that's necessary now if we are to revitalise our political institutions.

Jean McNicol: Rather than becoming MPs, people like you, Geoffrey Robertson and Michael Mansfield have become QCs. Do you think this is an indication that the Bar realises the necessity of change or do you think it's an attempt to co-opt you?

Helena Kennedy: Becoming a Queen's Counsel has in no way inhibited me from expressing my views about the judiciary, for example. I don't feel that taking silk has in any way interfered with my independence. One of the poisonous things within the British system is that in order to rise up the hierarchical ladder the people who determine whether you should rise are the judges – the people who are already in place and the people you appear in front of. So the great tragedy of it all is that many people who become QCs and whose next step on the ladder would be to become a High Court judge start tailoring their performances in order to obtain the strokings and approval of those they appear in front of. Once lawyers start doing that you are on a hiding to nothing: there is the corruption of the system. I can say to you now that becoming a judge is not high on my list of ambitions.

Jean McNicol: Obviously it's harder to appear in front of judges if you don't share their presuppositions and prejudices, and it must be harder for you to get your arguments across. You've said before that you would be a 'lousy' judge because you like taking sides, but clearly pretty much every judge has spent his or her professional career as a barrister taking sides [HK: I think I'm more honest than they are.] and when they become judges they are again going to take sides and to make judgments on the basis of sex, race and class. You became a QC accepting that you would be judged for that position by people whose ideas of merit you don't agree with because you think that you have more of a voice as a QC. It could be said that you should take the next step and become a judge as well to act as some kind of balance to the reactionary bias of the judiciary.

Helena Kennedy: That's a truly valid argument and one would like to see more and more people coming through who will quietly go about doing that. I don't really know what I want to do in five years' time, but I certainly know that now I want to be involved in law reform: I'm interested in policy, I'm interested in ways in which we can make the law more accessible, make it function better and I'm very interested in making judges more accountable. I know that I can say that and say it quite clearly as someone who is not involved with the judiciary. Once you are sitting as a judge you can't say that, you can't start turning round and saying that your colleagues shouldn't be there, you can't speak out like that.

Jean McNicol: Do you think that the appointment of Brenda Hoggett is an important one? [She is the first academic to be appointed to the English High Court without having practised law.]

Helena Kennedy: That's a terrific appointment. I'm absolutely thrilled about that, she's a very interesting woman. We've just recently seen some female appointments which I think are interesting appointments. In the initial stages the women who were appointed tended to be fairly disowning of their own sex and to deny that there was ever any prejudice and say that it was all about merit and that they happened to wear the badge of merit. Brenda Hoggett, however, wrote a very interesting book with Susan Atkins about women and the law from a very progressive perspective, and she is a woman who is very clear about the disadvantages that women have experienced and who knows how the law in different ways has entrenched that disadvantage. She's an academic lawyer, she hasn't practised and that is very important and I think we should have more of those appointments. There are a lot of very good academics who would enrich the Bench. Her appointment was a great delight.

Jean McNicol: Another woman in a very important and exposed position is Barbara Mills [HK: Another terrific woman.] who has had an awful lot of criticism. Women who enter male bastions tend to suffer a disproportionate amount of criticism in which their supposed weaknesses are said to be representative of those of their sex. Harriet Harman has been criticised as a Shadow Treasury spokesperson in a similar way.

Helena Kennedy: Absolutely. Women end up being much more visible and there are those traditionalists who are happy to find a rationale which proves that give a woman an inch and she takes a mile, give a woman an inch and she proves she shouldn't have been given half of it. There is always that problem for women. Barbara Mills is an incredibly capable woman and could have knocked spots off the vast majority of men at the Bar, and did. She also brought up four children, all of whom went through state education, had a very demanding career and has been terrific at it. She is also pushing for much better working conditions for women within the Crown Prosecution Service: she's actually introduced very clear equal opportunity guidelines in there. So this is a woman who is doing it for her own sex as well. She is interested in doing a number of quite progressive things. One is that she wants to give rights of audience to her own folk: there are arguments on both sides about whether that is a good thing or not, but she's certainly looking after her own people and making sure that their jobs are fulfilling and satisfying. In doing that, of course, she's going to make enemies of all those monopolistic organisations like the Bar from which she came, and so she's not going to have many friends on that side of the profession. Some solicitors themselves aren't happy about it because they see it as being a lot of work. She also strictly applies the 50/50 rule: if you haven't got a real chance of succeeding then why go through the business and waste public money, but of course the reactionary forces of law and order don't like that, they want everybody prosecuted up hill and down dale. You can't win on that, particularly just now when everybody is being encouraged to believe that if you put your big toe out of your front door you're going to be chopped into little pieces.

Jean McNicol: Do you think it makes any difference that the Lord Chancellor is Scottish?

Helena Kennedy: Absolutely, I have a high regard for him [Lord Mackay]: I think he was absolutely clear that he would not be subverted by the old mechanisms. He does not go along with the old boy network, which means he doesn't go along to the Garrick Club and have things whispered in his ear, he doesn't like that kind of thing. I think he's very ethical about it and very clear. I think that he's been a breath of fresh air in the way we do things and although he has this kind of orthodox Protestant idea that the buck stops with him, that his appointments to the Bench and to silk are all between him and God, it's still an improvement on Lord Hailsham whose appointments were between him and the small clique of judges that he bothered to confer with. I think what's happened with this Lord Chancellor is that he is much more formal in the way that he takes views from people, it's not just whispering behind hands. He has very regulated ways of doing it, he actually sends out a list to named individuals and while that's not acceptable either I think it certainly widens the scope more than anybody has done in the past, although the whole idea of doing things by taking soundings is not the way that it should be done at all and it will become much less possible as the potential for the Bench moves beyond just the Bar. When the Bar was a small profession in which everybody knew everybody, in some senses – if you were to rip away the prejudices – it might have actually been a way where everybody recognised who was good. But when you start having a wider intake which involves both solicitors and the academic world then you need a better mechanism that just honest gossip. He believes in meritocracy and I think he also believes that if people are good it shouldn't matter what side of the political divide they come from.

However, I'm very unhappy about what he's doing to legal aid, and that is the downside of this Protestant ethic. He believes that if you want to go to law you should be prepared to sell your car and to go without, that people shouldn't rely on the state. He believes in the deserving and undeserving poor and I don't like that side of his approach. But there's no doubt that when Maggie was looking for a man who would reform the legal profession, it could not have been one of the old guard. None of these boys in Parliament who come from the Bar would in any way have dealt a blow to their own profession. It's a club: it's like voting for Jeremy Paxman to join the Garrick, you either are in line or you're out of line, they wouldn't have done it. So she brought in an outsider.

Jean McNicol: The Bar now has committees dealing with race and sex discrimination and has to abide by legislation on these matters, thanks largely to the work people like you have done. How much difference have these committees made and do you think people take them seriously?

Helena Kennedy: Attitudes have to change before you get anywhere, but they sometimes don't change unless you have sticks to beat people with. What we found at the Bar was that first of all they didn't believe that there was any problem at all either for women or blacks, and you had to provide great bodies of evidence actually to prove it to them, where anyone with half a brain could see that there were problems. Once it was proved that there was discrimination we had to put in place methods to redress that. Of course there was no way we were going to be able to introduce positive discrimination, although men have been the beneficiaries of that from the year dot. For women we had to make sure that there weren't any unacceptable practices in interviewing candidates – asking them if they were getting married or on the Pill. Black people were being discriminated against by just not getting places in chambers. There are now targets, not quotas, for chambers to try to improve their performance when it comes to race and we're trying to get a maternity policy in place for women. What you do is that you raise these issues until they are taken as read and new generations will come up that will not have the attitudes of the old ones.

Jean McNicol: You are known as a supporter of the cab-rank rule. Stephen Sedley has said that this principle, in which barristers should be willing to accept any client, is actually operated on the same basis as a cab-driver's treatment of a passenger not going his way. In other words, many barristers have never adhered to it and would never do legal aid cases or represent suspected terrorists.

Helena Kennedy: When the Lord Chancellor decided he would take away a lot of the monopolistic rights of the Bar this meant that the Bar had to stand up and justify its existence. One of the ways it did this was by declaring its commitment to the cab-rank rule, which meant that it suddenly had to start pulling into line all those people who said, for example, that they didn't do legal aid work. What it means, of course, is that they are just not available to do it; there are other ways of getting round it. They also made it very clear that there was no question of saying: 'I'm not going to represent certain kinds of defendant'. There will always be people who will find ways round the rules, we know that, but I think the principle that one is not going to start picking and choosing between defendants because one has a view on the nature of the offence or on the likelihood that they might well have committed it is crucial to the role of the advocate. Once we start doing that it's a very dangerous road. It means, you see, that if, for example, I start saying that I will not represent anybody who's charged with rape, it suggests that people who are representing those charged with rape are automatically on the side of people who commit those offences.

Jean McNicol: Like the case of the Irish barrister Patrick Finucane who defended IRA suspects and was killed by Loyalist terrorists.

Helena Kennedy: They assumed that he must be a supporter of the IRA, and there are all sorts of rather foolish people who assume the same sorts of things about any of us who have been involved in representing those charged with terrorist offences, and make the assumption that we are 'soft' on terrorism. In the early days when people like Mike Mansfield and myself spoke out publicly about our concerns about things having gone wrong in Irish cases we were accused of being soft on terrorism when in fact what one was soft on was justice. We were concerned about civil liberties and concerned about the failure of the system. But that's what happens when these crude correlations are made.

Jean McNicol: Do you think rape trials are handled any differently when you are representing the defendant?

Helena Kennedy: You don't have to put the woman to trial in order to conduct a rape trial properly and for the most part the men who are defending these cases are doing things that are uncalled for. It has to be possible to say that there is a different way of doing it, so it's for me in some way to show that you can do these cases and do them properly without having to abuse the person who is making the complaint. I think there's a challenge to us as women or as people concerned about the law's failings to show how it can be done properly, and I think it's nihilistic to say: 'Well, I'm just not going to do it'. I remember in the early days when this big argument was really running high in the women's movement on whether one should do this kind of case or not, the opposition was almost invariably by women who were not criminal defence lawyers. I also remember one of my colleagues saying: 'It's very hard to decide whether I'd rather have my legs blown off or whether I'd rather be raped'. Many of the people who would have said that terrorists had to be defended were the ones saying that people charged with rape shouldn't be, or that other people should do it. Once you start saying that it's the responsibility of other people I think you're being hypocritical.

Jean McNicol: I suppose at the moment rape defendants must feel it bolsters their case to have a woman defending them. If more women did defend rapists it would presumably lose this novelty value and be less of an advantage than it is now.

Helena Kennedy: I think that undoubtedly at the moment male defendants in those sexually-based crimes can benefit from having a woman represent them, but that will pass fairly quickly because of the numbers of women coming into the law now and it will move on from that. But it can't be a rationale for saying that women shouldn't be doing it.

Jean McNicol: You've written about it being easier to get the judge and the jury's sympathy for a woman defendant who is a conventional, stereotypical wife and mother. To represent your clients' best interests you have to encourage them to feminise themselves. Is this successful and how do you deal with the problem that to get the best treatment for women you have to reinforce stereotypical ideas about them?

Helena Kennedy: I always make the joke about how one has been driven at times to say to one's female clients: turn up in an angora sweater or wear a broderie anglaise blouse and cover up your tattoos and dispense with your bovver boots, but I would never say that to a woman without explaining to her what it was all about and giving her the choice. It's important that women feel entitled to say: 'Damn it, I'm not going to play that game'. The real responsibility you have as a lawyer, I believe, is that you're giving voice to your client's case in the way that they would themselves if they were able to, and had the skills or the training. There's an obligation to work very much hand in hand with the person you're representing, so I always say to women: 'Look, this is how it is, I think the risks are that you are going to be judged because you are a lesbian woman or because you are a woman who's confronting expectations about how women should behave. We can ameliorate that by, if you like, confusing the signals by the way you present yourself.' The choices have to be theirs but well-informed by you and in sympathy with whatever their aim will be, and knowing that you'll support them whatever they decide to do. I've had women decide it either way; all the Greenham women that I represented said: 'Sod it, I will not play that game', and didn't, and lost.

Jean McNicol: Of course they were women who had a very strong political agenda and who believed in what they were doing. It's much easier not to compromise if you have that strength of purpose, when being found guilty could almost be construed as the aim of your actions. It must, however, be depressing knowing that you get better results if you collude in infantilising, domesticising, feminising and medicalising women.

Helena Kennedy: There are ways in which inevitably one colludes in attitudes which are undermining of women because, as I always say to people, there is nothing too terrific about going to prison, and at the end of the day I will do what I have to do to reduce the risks of my clients going to prison, whether they are male or female. I reconcile myself to the contradictions, but one should never become blind to them, forget they exist, and I think that, unfortunately, and not just in my profession, too many people by the repetition stop realising that that's what's happening.

Jean McNicol: You've just mentioned prisons. One of the things that surprised me in your book was how many women are sent to prison; the number of black women especially is quite shocking. [29 per cent of the female prison population in England and Wales are black; 13 per cent are foreign women imprisoned for drug offences.]

Helena Kennedy: I go into Holloway Prison from time to time, not just to see clients, but also because of projects I'm involved with in the prison and there's nothing more awful than the fact that there are weeks when the majority of women there are black being incarcerated by a vast majority of women who are white. There's something horribly imperialistic about it and it has to make us ask ourselves questions about what's going on in our society. It is shocking, and I hope it's shocking because once we stop being shocked. . . .

Jean McNicol: Michael Howard, of course, thinks we should put more people in prison.

Helena Kennedy: What makes me so cross is that he's a lawyer; he should know better. I don't know if he's ever set foot in a criminal court in his life or seen the inside of a prison. Probably not. But how dare these people talk about criminality in that way! It's about cheap electioneering. On the one hand they talk about family values and yet, if you want to see families being destroyed, visit our prisons, speak to the children of prisoners. You're considered a bleeding heart if you talk about the social price that's paid for these things and how we're creating a cycle of deprivation, a new generation whose pain will ultimately manifest itself in crime or in self-destruction of some sort. There is such blindness and such willingness to exploit the fears of the general public at a time of recession when there's economic anxiety anyway; to exploit fears about crime in order to justify your own existence, because that's what they're doing, trying to hang on to power. It makes me look back to Margaret Thatcher, who was ideologically driven but somehow, despite the fact that one thought she was awful, and perhaps the mother of all this ghastliness and the mother of this crowd of ghastly men who are now running the show, there's something even more awful about this crowd, who are driven by nothing except the desire to remain in power.

Jean McNicol: Women in court, victims as well as perpetrators, suffer from the division into good and bad women: you don't count so much if you're raped or murdered if you're a prostitute, as in the Yorkshire Ripper case. Women are supposed to react in specific ways if they've been abused or raped or something has happened to their children. They're supposed to cry, calmness is suspicious. You've said that the use of the question 'why didn't she leave?' is indicative of the lack of understanding of the position of female victims.

Helena Kennedy: It's always about blaming women: women who are battered must be exaggerating what happened to them. It's always why didn't she leave, why did she go out late at night, why was she dressed the way she was, why didn't she say 'no' clearly, why did she allow him to kiss her . . . It's always a criticism of the woman and from that we can even have the eight-year-old little girl being blamed for her own sexual assault. Why do women keep working for a man who is sexually harassing them . . . ?

Jean McNicol: Obviously a lot of this has to do with class as well.

Helena Kennedy: Of course. The more one deals with all those things the more one recognises that class is such a problem in Britain. The resolution of all this business to do with women will not come about until we resolve the business of class. I see it in my profession where there have been women who succeeded in the law, and I look around me and there are a number of my contemporaries at my stage and many of them managed to do it because their children were sent away to boarding school when they were seven. Once you've got your children off your hands at seven and sent them into those monstrous places then you just function like a single woman, or a single man for that matter, and you're well enough off to have the support systems that ensure that you don't have to do anything domestic. You just function in the way that privileged women have always been able to by sub-contracting all the female stuff. The new generations of women who are coming up are having to deal with the contradictions: they want to be mothers, they want to have first-hand involvement with their children and childcare, they want their menfolk to have that too, but they also want to have a career. That's posing the big challenge and, of course, one doesn't want to be doing it at the expense of other women in an exploitative way, so there are many more problems for the new generation of women who are trying to do things differently.

Jean McNicol: I read one or two interviews you'd done including one for the 'Day in the Life' section of the *Sunday Times* [HK: which I greatly regret] which was probably a mistake because it's so easy with women in your position for your words to make you sound like you're a fraud. You're asked a lot more questions about your partner and your children than a man would be, and there almost seems to be an attempt to defuse the threat to the established order they might see posed by your opinions by making you sound like a bourgeois Hampstead woman in a big white house formerly owned by R. D. Laing.

Helena Kennedy: Yes, who has a nanny to look after her children. There are all these problems, as we were discussing when we talked about Barbara Mills, that women are exposed to but men are not. Nobody ever asks men how they manage their childcare or their home, and men are never expected to explain that in fact you end up feeling that you do not do any of these things the way you would like to. In the 'Day in the Life' piece one of the things I'd wanted to do was make it clear to people that there are no Superwomen and that you may do all of these things, but it's only because you're in a privileged position once you've gone into a profession where you can afford to have help. What made me laugh was that afterwards the *New Statesman* had a little gibe about it, you know, what are you supposed to do? Here am I representing people facing life imprisonment, can you imagine that I would be able to say to the judge, 'I'm terribly sorry, Your Lordship, but I'm late today because my nanny had the flu'. You have to somehow make it fit with the responsibilities and the problems that come with a particular line of work, but if you're a journalist on the *New Statesman* I'm sure you can phone up the editor and say, 'Sorry, I won't be in today', but you can't do that at the Old Bailey when your client's on a murder charge.

Jean McNicol: The police have traditionally been unwilling to get involved in things like domestic violence which happen in the private sphere, but they are willing to interfere in that sphere in cases like Operation Spanner [where the convictions of gay men involved in consensual and private sado-masochistic sex were upheld by the House of Lords].

Helena Kennedy: For a very long time the private domain was deemed to be a no-go area for the police, and women and children suffered the consequences of that. Somehow one almost feels that because we as women have opened up that privacy domain and said it shouldn't be a no-go area, it has to be an area into which the police are prepared to go, we have if you like opened up a gate which it turns out the police can use in the way that they have. I think you have to recognise that some of the gains that we have made as feminists have a downside in the bigger civil liberties arena. I have no doubt that it was the women's movement which opened up the debate about how women were being treated in the courts and from that there developed an analysis of the experience of the victim, which grew into a look at how children experience the courtroom and we have seen changes in the law in relation to that. But that development of the victim lobby has meant that we now have the law and order crowd jumping on the back of that and saying let's up the rights of victims and reduce the rights of defendants, so that the right to silence is lost, they're not given bail, get long sentences and so on and the argument is always made that this is because of the poor victim. In some ways it's about ways in which very important moves by us as women can be hijacked, ways in which we find ourselves being bedfellows rather uncomfortably with those on the Right, and so we have to make it very clear that we are talking about something different.

Jean McNicol: The formal equality of the law, of course, can disguise the fact that it has more impact on some groups than on others. The provocation defence in murder cases, for example, is one more easily made by men. Cumulative provocation is a defence in Australia and many people would like to see it introduced here. Do you think there is a danger in a law which might seem to legitimise revenge and which could rebound on women?

Helena Kennedy: Absolutely. What I say to people is don't automatically look for legislative change as the remedy. A better way of doing it is to insist on the contextualising of offences in the courtroom, making sure that judges are summing up properly to juries about how the past can inform the present, and that the history may be an important feature of a case. That is a much more sensible way forward than actually creating legislative change which could have the downside of meaning that there would be people who would take advantage of a looser law to justify killing.

Jean McNicol: You've always argued against gender-specific defences.

Helena Kennedy: I've kind of reconciled myself to it, but I was very unhappy about using the language of Battered Woman's Syndrome because I think that it does pathologise women. I was much keener that we just recognised that where there has been long-term abuse any of us may end up bearing the psychological consequences of that, which may provide us with a defence because it would fall within the diminished responsibility definition. I was unhappy about making it seem specific to women because there's no doubt that if men were treated in the same way they would have the same psychological manifestations and symptoms. Unfortunately, some of the fellows were quite keen to use it, and did, and it has taken hold and the judges now use the term themselves.

Jean McNicol: You wrote in *Eve Was Framed* that you had seen rape trials very well conducted in the States. I read a piece by Catharine MacKinnon [radical feminist and professor of law at the University of Michigan] recently in which she asserted that 'sexual assault in the US resembles lynching prior to its recognition as a civil rights violation'. Do you find this kind of totalising feminist writing difficult to deal with?

Helena Kennedy: I don't think there's any way forward either in alienating other women who may not have quite the same perspective and who are coming to grips with these ideas slowly or in alienating men. I just think one has to be persuasive and I've written in true advocate's style of trying to win people to the argument rather than make them hostile to it. I think an awful lot of feminist dialogue has been hostile and unhelpful and I'm afraid I think Catharine does not always help.

Jean McNicol: There has been a lot of discussion about date rape recently with the Austin Donnellan case and the publication of a book dismissing it as a manifestation of 'victim feminism' by a young American called Katie Roiphe. Why do you think people want to make out that there is a qualitative distinction between date rape and the classic notion of rape as being something inflicted on a woman by a stranger in a back alley?

Helena Kennedy: I think that most people have been in a situation like the date rape scenario – if not quite then getting there – and certainly lots of men have been in the situation where they've persuaded somebody into sexual intercourse against their will. The closer it gets to the general experience the more uncomfortable people are and the more they want to turn it into something that's normal and ordinary. Most men know that they don't go around holding a knife at people's throats and forcing themselves on them. People want to distinguish between violent violation and persuading women to have sex when they don't really want to. I think that you can't start fudging the legal definition, it's very clear and simple: it's about non-consensual sexual relations. It's like the old legal joke about tax evasion and tax avoidance being the same as rape and seduction. Most people think that seduction is about persuading someone to part with something that they don't really want to part with, or that they don't know whether they want to part with or not. It still feeds back into the idea that women don't know their own minds, that women don't really like sex and therefore have to be persuaded to participate in it, but that they like it once you've done it – that ghastly old-fashioned game plan which I think is less and less how young people conduct their sexual lives. We don't date in this country, God, dating is an American invention of going out specially . . . People in this country more often than not meet people at work or by studying with them or being friends with them and then slowly it turns into something else. We don't have that dating tradition that they have there, which is all intent on one thing.

Jean McNicol: Katie Roiphe's book is about being at Yale . . .

Helena Kennedy: All these fraternity clubs and all that ghastly stuff where collecting cherries is the main aim in life. Happily we don't conduct ourselves quite in that way. But double sexual standards still exist: we still somehow have expectations of women which are very different from those we have of men, that women shouldn't be putting it around. Even although we've got over the belief that women have to be virgins or married and we don't expect that any more, promiscuity still means something different for women than for men. Women have to be able to say 'no' even when they have been quite intimate with somebody, kissing and necking. Juries deal with the individual facts in the case and there will always be a problem where you are talking about one person's word against another's, whatever the nature of the case; if the standard of proof is high then there's going to be a higher acquittal rate in rape than in other things because the offence is in private. It's also difficult when people are sending out signals that might be confusing, but juries will weigh all that up and if they're left in doubt they will acquit. There are large stretches of the women's movement who will feel unhappy about that in certain cases, but the same thing happens in other areas of crime too, and we want the burden of proof to be high because we don't want people found guilty too easily because we are talking about the liberty of the subject. There are consequences for all of us if we start changing the rules for particular kinds of offence. I think that the definition of rape is fine except that it could be extended to include anal penetration; it's extraordinary that penile penetration is the only thing that counts. Of course we created that at the time when it was all about pregnancy, about male seed, and about the stealing of woman as property. In this age we are really talking about it being a violation of the most private parts of one's being, and I think that forcing oneself into someone anally should be of the same order. I also think you could take away the gender issue, it could be genderless; homosexual rape takes place too.

Jean McNicol: Do you think there is much difference in the way criminal law works in Scotland, where it's based on common law not statute-based as it is in England?

Helena Kennedy: Undoubtedly there are a lot of much better things about the Scottish criminal law. I think the two sources rule is a very good one and we might not have got into the same mess on confessions had it existed. The only thing is that I don't think it's good enough for Scottish lawyers to be complacent: Scotland hasn't had to face terrorism in the same way. When you have these sort of strong emotions aroused in any system there's a risk that people start sacrificing high standards and that the rules get broken. I think that the procurator fiscal system is a very good other tier within the prosecuting process which I think it would be very good to introduce here; the 110 day rule: all terrific things. I am not happy about 'not proven' verdicts: I don't like them, it leaves a stigma and there are cases where people should really have been acquitted. One must never allow oneself to be smug about one's system, thinking it's terrific. When I'm in Scotland, Scottish lawyers, male lawyers usually, say to me that there's no problem in rape cases there, but what women tell me is that all the same problems in attitudes, sometimes with bells on, exist in Scotland. The recent work done on whether judges allowed cross-examination about the victim's sexual history totally replicated what was happening down here.

Jean McNicol: Scottish judges in rape cases don't have to give the statutory warning to the jury about the dangers of relying solely on the woman's evidence.

Helena Kennedy: No, that's right, at least they don't have that ugly business of having to say that women are hysterical and they make these things up. There are lots of far better things about the Scottish system, but it's all about attitudes. When I was in New Zealand at a big conference of women judges there were all these wonderful women from all over the world, and what they always say is that when you talk about discrimination in somebody's system people always say, 'That happens in Australia, but it doesn't happen here in New Zealand' or they say in Canada, 'Oh, that happens in the United States, but it doesn't happen here in Canada'; people always say it's fine in my place, but these awful things go on elsewhere. And the Scots always say that all these terrible things go on down in England, and English people say to me that it's much worse up in Scotland because they're much more dyed in the wool. We mustn't imagine that these things are the personal property of any particular nation.

CATRIONA BURNESS

Drunk Women Don't Look At Thistles: Women and the SNP, 1934–94

'The SNP has always encouraged women to play an active part in politics'[1], suggested journalist Jean Donald in 1978. Yet the role of women in the SNP is an aspect of Scottish nationalism which has certainly been overlooked by historians. The aim of this paper is to begin to explore the extent of a 'tradition' which associates the Scottish National Party (SNP) and women. The conclusions arrived at are tentative, indicating findings from research undertaken to date. Discussion focuses on four areas: firstly, women's activities in the forerunner of the SNP, the National Party of Scotland (NPS); secondly, the SNP's wilderness years, 1934–1967; thirdly, the impact of electoral breakthrough from 1967; and lastly, the likely future involvement of women in the SNP. Most of the comment on women's representation relates to the parliamentary level and the party's record on putting up women as parliamentary candidates will be compared with that of other parties.

The discussion has to be set into the context of women's historic under-representation at Westminster. In 1992 60 women MPs were elected to the House of Commons, a record level of 9.2%, since increased at by-elections to 62 women MPs, that is, 9.5%. Scotland has also reached a record level of 8.3%, returning six women MPs. The previous highest levels of Scottish women's representation occurred in 1959, 1964 and 1992 with the return of five Scottish women MPs, that is, 7%. Since Westminster opened to women in 1918 only 23 women – 13 Labour, six Conservative, three SNP and one Liberal Democrat – have represented Scottish constituencies. In most European countries there has been a continuing upward trend since 1945 particularly in the Scandinavian countries such as Norway and Sweden.[2] The upward trend in Norway and Sweden has been most marked since the beginning of the 1970s when major parties in those countries adopted quota systems to make sure that a certain proportion of parliamentary candidates was female. In Scotland and the UK instead of a gradual upward trend there has been a pattern of rise and fall within a low level.

Yet the percentage of women MPs as a percentage of the total of Scottish

MPs returned has been marginally higher than the UK average at 14 of the 21 general elections that have taken place since 1918.[3] Since 1979, however, Scotland has returned a lesser proportion of women to Westminster than the UK average. This fact has been underlined by increasing awareness of far higher levels of women's representation outside of Scotland and the UK and appears to have given rise to a widespread impression that Scotland has always had a worse record than the UK average on women's representation.[4] This impression in fact already existed in 1979. Margaret Bain (now Ewing), then the former MP for Dumbarton East, took issue with it in 1980:

> Myths abound that Scotland is a chauvinistic country – of the male chauvinistic pig variety . . . and that Scotswomen face greater difficulties in getting to Parliament. *Machismo*, it is argued, is a greater trial than selection boards. Yet Scotland's record in electing women Members of Parliament is better than that of the UK as a whole. One hundred and nine women have trod the corridors of power . . . sixteen of them from Scotland. That is a proportion which far exceeds the old Goschen population percentage formula . . .[5]

Given the idea of '*machismo*' as peculiarly Scottish chauvinism and the related although separate question of the continuing polemical, political and literary debate around the elusive concept of 'Scottish national identity', brief reference is also made to the marginalisation of women from this debate. This debate is set into the context of the experience of women in other nationalist movements.

WOMEN AND THE NATIONAL PARTY OF SCOTLAND (NPS)

The formation of the NPS in 1928 brought together the existing nationalist societies, the Scots League, the Scottish National Movement, the Home Rule Association and the University Nationalist Association. The party rapidly took on such electoral challenge as their limited resources allowed, putting up the poet Lewis Spence as their first candidate at the Midlothian and Peebleshire by-election in January 1929 and putting up two candidates at the so-called 'flapper election' of 1929. Any expectations of rapid electoral headway were dashed by the results which gave them a top poll of only 5.4% of the votes cast.[6] The 1929 election campaign, however, gives some indication of appeals to women. As early as October 1927 the *Scots Independent* had promised future 'articles written by Scotswomen on subjects of special interest to womankind'[7] but the first piece of any substance relating to women was written by Rhoda Spence in anticipation of the 1929 election.

She attacked those who patronised the new women voters, '"How Will the Women Vote?" they ask, much, one feels, in the same spirit as they might enquire, "How will the Lunatic Asylums Vote?"' In developing her appeal to women, 'one of the most vital and intelligent portions of the Scottish electorate', she related poor living conditions and the 'deplorable exodus' of emigration to 'the evils and neglect attendant upon government from a point 400 miles distant'. Scottish women, she noted, had been described as 'realists', and added, 'the reason for that is not far to seek. In Scotland today they are **compelled** to face realities, especially in those homes where the weekly budget rests entirely in the housewife's hands, and she is faced with the continual struggle for a bare existence under conditions which are an affront to any civilised nation'.[8]

Her solution naturally lay in a Scottish Parliament, and her appeal ended with a tribute to the courage and endurance of Scottish women in the past – 'Can it be that their patriotism and fineness has no echo in the hearts of Scotswomen today? I cannot believe that it is so'.[9] This appeal was in keeping with a 1922 Scottish Home Rule Association pamphlet, 'A Point for Women Voters', which described Scottish national self-government as 'the reform which includes all others' and 'which will help [women] in the rule of the home and the control of their industrial lives'.[10] The patriotic appeal reappeared in 'Aunt Jean's Advice to Women Voters' in April 1929. Three young girls – Jeanie, Flora and Elspeth – sought Aunt Jean's advice on how to vote:

> 'Why vote **Party** at all?' said Mrs Gemmell quietly when thus appealed to. "Why not vote for the **Nation**, as **Nationalists**? The nation is immeasurably greater than any party, and it needs all the help anyone can give it. You are all Scots; there isn't one of you who does not love your country, nor one who does not see, as I do, how much it has suffered under past governments: Tory, Liberal and Labour. What do they care for Scotland; it is nothing but a pawn in the game to them? . . . Is it not time, think you, to have done with parties; to think rather of the interests of your native land and its people – your own kith and kin?'[11]

'Aunt Jean's' folksy appeal was essentially a nationalist variation on 'down-to-earth' appeals made to women voters by all the parties, most typically addressing women as wives and mothers.[12] This competitive appeal to women voters reflected a period of intense inter-party struggle within which the nationalists scarcely figured. The outcome of this conflict saw the beginning of the long-term decline of the Liberal Party and the rise of the Labour Party. The Conservatives (fighting as Unionists in Scotland) reaped the benefit of the party struggle as the dominant party of the inter-war period. While the NPS and later the SNP arguably did succeed in 'keeping alive an issue that was exclusively Scottish and which helped to maintain a peculiarly "national" dimension in Scotland's political life',[13] their impact on general elections was severely limited. The 1929 election found nationalists adopting pressure group tactics outside of the two seats contested by NPS candidates. 'NW', who described herself as a former Secretary of a Women's Society of over a thousand members (non-party), suggested a course of action for women in 'The Woman's Election: How We Must Help':

> Get your question . . . put on paper, have it put to each candidate and insist on a reply. Failing all these, go yourself; even if you have to go alone, one lone woman, GO! But a small group is best (three is perhaps the ideal number) . . .
> . . . During the election of 1918 . . . we followed the methods I have sketched above, and they answered. The men who were asking us for our votes paid attention!
> The form of the question might well be . . . . 'Are you in favour of the reconstruction of Scottish National life, including self-government for Scotland, with independent status within the British group of nations?'[14]

There are other indications that the NPS was keen to involve women. In October 1928 the *Scots Independent* reported the appointment of John MacGregor as the Party's National Organiser and added, 'It is hoped that, in a short while, the appointment of a special Women's Organiser will also be made. There is great need of such an official and . . . it is earnestly requested that all readers will favourably consider the [financial] appeal which accompanies this paper'.[15] Whether or not the NPS did appoint its Women's Organiser is unclear from subsequent editions of the *Scots Independent* but an early member Muriel Gibson describes being persuaded to join the NPS rather than the Scottish Party in 1932 by a Miss Judith Allan, the National Party organiser.[16] In January 1929 it was reported from Kinghorn, Burntisland, and Kirkcaldy that a meeting held in Lady Lockhart's home had led to a Women's Section being formed with Lady Lockhart as President.[17] The *Scots Independent* credited Elma Campbell, later to be the first woman parliamentary candidate for the NPS, with building the women's organisation:

> We wonder how often the introduction of a woman into the normal order of things has called for an entire re-arrangement of ideas. When the 'Men in the Movement' some eighteen months ago had to accept the advent of a woman's section under the brilliant leadership of Miss

Elma Campbell, it was soon patent to all that in courage, enthusiasm and ability they had met their equal – if not their superior.[18]

The organisation, however, was perhaps not too securely founded as in April 1932 Catriona Cameron of Glasgow called 'a meeting of Scotswomen . . . to see what could be done about the formation of a Women's Movement, as it was felt that something more should be done to further the cause of self-government among women'. Around eighty women were served a menu of speeches, tea, songs and violin solos after which thirty women joined.[19] Clearly there were several attempts to develop organisation among women. These efforts now appear to be almost entirely forgotten, not least by present day SNP women activists.

Branch reports to the *Scots Independent* give other indications of women's activity within the party at large. Ninety-nine local NPS branches and secretaries were listed in August 1932. Not every listing indicated an active branch – 'Some of the places . . . have at present only a local correspondent or a committee as a nucleus of further development'. Fifteen of the local branch secretaries were women. The branches were organised in ten areas or federations; of nine federation or area secretaries named, one was a woman, Catriona Cameron, Secretary of the West Renfrewshire Federation (although she lived in Glasgow).[20] The branch reports also indicate women's emergence as speakers and apparently as election agents – for instance, Catriona Cameron reported on election co-ordination in West Renfrewshire during the 1931 general election,[21] while 'the excellent and self-sacrificing work of Miss Jean S Fraser' during the Montrose Burghs by-election in 1932 was commended.[22]

Elma Campbell was the exception as the only nationalist woman parliamentary candidate of the inter-war years. She stood for parliament twice in Glasgow St Rollox, first, at the by-election of May 1931 and then at the general election later that year. A former Glasgow University Conservative debating champion she had risen rapidly on joining the NPS. In 1930 she was Joint Convenor of the Women's Section, member of the organisation, finance, press and publications, and bazaar committees, and the National Council. She was credited with being 'one of our most brilliant speakers', having addressed audiences of 'over four thousand in St Andrew's Halls, Glasgow'.[23] Her by-election poll of 15.8% and general election poll of 13.3% of the votes cast were among the best nationalist results up to that point.[24] A teacher in Greenock, she was refused leave of absence during both campaigns. It was remarked that 'the amount of work put in was simply astonishing when one considers that the candidate attended on average seven meetings each night'.

Her marriage to Thomas Gibson in March 1932 and his employment in London removed both from the Scottish political scene. Otherwise she might well have contested other elections for the SNP during the 1930s. Her focus was very much on nationalism per se, and her interest in women's activities seems to have been organisational, and not in women's issues as such. In this she is much like later leading nationalist women.

This account of women's activity in the NPS appears to locate most women in local organising roles – but not only behind the teapot. It is important to keep in mind, however, that the party was small and, in electoral terms, a dismal failure. By 1939 SNP membership had shrunk from 10,000 in 1934 to less than 2,000.[25] This account is also unrelated to women's roles in the controversies which actually engulfed the party throughout the inter-war years and beyond. Women such as Wendy Wood were undoubtedly controversial and conspicuous.

WILDERNESS YEARS

The sidelining (via expulsion) of the party's more flamboyant and excessive literary leading lights such as Christopher Grieve did not dramatically transform electoral prospects for the SNP. Despite Dr Robert McIntyre's short-lived victory at the 1945 Motherwell by-election the party's vote at general elections did not rise above 30,000 until 1964.[26] Support for the Scottish Covenant clearly demonstrated the paradox that has bedevilled political nationalism in Scotland, whereby support for a measure of Scottish self-determination has not meant electoral support for the SNP. By 1951 more than two million people had signed the Covenant, pledging themselves 'to do everything in our power to secure for Scotland a Parliament with adequate legislative authority in Scottish affairs'.[27] The Covenant itself diverted potential nationalist recruits. Hanham thought that the SNP's great achievement from 1942 to 1964 was 'simply to have survived'.[28]

Muriel Gibson commented that 'Nationalists were treated as fanatics in the 1930s. We were called the "fanatic fringe"'.[29] The position altered little after 1945. Highland activist Nancy Forsyth explained, 'To be a patriot and a nationalist was "not the thing to be", especially in the 50s and 60s. It was not considered "respectable"'.[30] These comments reflect the fringe nature of SNP activity during these years. According to Hanham, during the late 40s and 50s the campaign strategy of the party was 'to keep up the momentum . . . by concentrating on municipal elections and by fighting parliamentary elections only in places where the party was already well established'.[31]

Further research would be required to establish how many women candidates stood for local government positions. At the parliamentary level only one woman contested a seat for the SNP between 1931 and 1967. That was Mary Dott, a founder member of the party, who stood in the Edinburgh East by-election of 1947. The selection of other women candidates was perhaps inhibited by the unfounded but widespread view expressed by Oliver Brown that 'Any party boss knows that a woman candidate will forfeit several thousand votes at an election because of the anti-feminine prejudices of the women voters'.[32] Mary Dott also became one of a series of women National Secretaries of the party. Former SNP candidate Maureen Watt has speculated on the reasons behind this female succession:

> We have also had women National Secretaries for as long as I can remember until fairly recently. I wonder why women like Christine MacWhirter and Muriel Gibson were elected to that position. Was it because it was then seen as secretarial? Now all of these posts are attracting media attention and now these posts are being filled by men.[33]

The nationalist woman most likely to attract press attention before 1967 was certainly Wendy Wood. An active Home Ruler since 1916 she became a founder member of the NPS in 1928. Her autobiography states that 'From then on I worked like mad for it, but all in a very humble way, scrubbing floors of committee rooms, giving out leaflets, getting new members . . .'.[34] Her gift of oratory was discovered when Lewis Spence conscripted her to stand in for an absent speaker and she became a regular platform performer. She acknowledged that speaking was 'the one gift I can offer to my country (it certainly is not organising!)'[35] In 1931 she commented 'What a spate of speaking a General Election brings! The year (1931) when John MacCormick first stood for Inverness, I was birled about in a car till I had to think twice what town I was in'.[36] By 1938, however, she was 'not allowed to speak at any big rally or at Bannockburn'[37] for the SNP. Her increasing involvement in symbolic acts of protest such as the raising of the Saltire at Stirling Castle drew the wrath of more moderate nationalists. Anne Raitt recalled: 'Mary Dott was furious with Wendy over the flag incident . . . but whatever Wendy Wood did got a lot of publicity at a time when the party couldn't get publicity. Not that she asked permission of the party!'[38]

Wendy Wood resigned from the SNP in 1946 to fight the Bridgeton by-election as an Independent Nationalist. Her later activities in running the Scottish Patriot organisation kept her on the outer fringes of nationalism. Oliver Brown commented that 'The strange thing about Wendy Wood's popularity is that it is greater among the women in her audiences than among the men'.[39] The extent of women's resistance to other women's political roles is an area for more detailed exploration in the future. Wendy Wood's impact on the SNP is problematic. She herself understood 'the

SNP's preference that I should be outside their ranks, since I had whiles jumped in with both feet where angels fear to tread'.[40] Some, like Nancy Forsyth, found her an inspiration: 'There are 3 "WWs" who have had a deep influence on my political thinking. The first is William Wallace, guardian of Scotland and patriot; the second is Wendy Wood, a patriot; and the third is William Wolfe, a nationalist . . .'.[41]

Wendy Wood failed in her aim of acting as a one-woman catalyst for Scottish independence – although not for the lack of trying! Yet others had far more to do with the nationalist breakthrough which occurred during the 1960s.

HAMILTON AND SCOTLAND'S 'HOME RULE HOUSEWIFE'

The 1960s brought several indications that the SNP was becoming a more serious political force. The failure of the Scottish Covenant Association to produce a consensus measure of Scottish self-government reclaimed the initiative for the SNP. By 1960 too, as Webb noted, 'for the first time, they found themselves to be both the standard-bearers of nationalism and a united party'.[42] The growth of the SNP during the 1960s was 'almost legendary'. From less than two thousand in 1962 party membership grew rapidly: 42,000 in November 1966; 50,000 in March 1967; to 100,000 in April 1968. The number of local branches rose from 21 in 1962 to 472 by 1968.[43]

Alongside this the number of SNP candidates increased at each election: five in 1959; 15 in 1964; and 23 in 1966.[44] In electoral terms came the decline of Scottish Unionism. The Scottish Unionist vote fell from 1,349,298 in 1951 to 960,654 by 1966; Unionist seats were cut from 36 in 1955 to 20 in 1966. This trend was accompanied by an erosion of the Labour vote. As Hanham put it, 'All over Britain there was a flight from Labour, which in Scotland assumed surprising proportions and culminated in the loss of one of the safest Labour seats in the House of Commons at Hamilton in 1967 and in an unprecedented clear-out of Labour town councillors in 1968'.[45]

The impact of the Hamilton by-election was electrifying; as the victor, Winnie Ewing, puts it, 'a real turn-up for the books':

> The advice I was given was 'try to come a good second' . . . I was selected as early as July 1966 in anticipation of an earlier by-election . . . [so] I was a by-election candidate for a whole year without a by-election. I worked very hard in the constituency attending Women's Guilds and fetes. I was given some very good publicity from a sympathetic journalist on the *Evening Times* and generally getting my face known . . .
> . . . When I won I really was in the press. Journalists were camped out in Queen's Drive in Glasgow to try to photo the children going to

school. There was a distinct feeling of celebration in the air . . .
. . . The *Hamilton Advertiser* had to change its front page for the result.
The headline was 'Winnie Wins by a Mile!'[46]

Some commentators found 'a sort of inevitability about what was happening, though we did not expect such a big drop in the Labour vote'.[47] Activist Ruth Marr underlines the importance of the Pollok by-election in March 1967 – 'A lot of young people joined the SNP during the Pollok by-election campaign in 1967 . . . Winnie Ewing has said, and I totally agree with her, we couldn't have won Hamilton without Pollok showing what could have been done'.[48] The Hamilton result transformed perceptions of the SNP and Margaret Ewing recalls this time as 'very heady . . . It projected the SNP as a credible political party . . . Plaid Cymru in Wales were also making a breakthrough at the same time and Gwynfor Evans was returned for Carmarthen just before Winnie won Hamilton. Nationalism was a new dynamic movement with repercussions for the whole political system'.[49]

The outcome left Winnie Ewing carrying the heavy weight of nationalist aspirations. Her preparations for her maiden speech took place in a blaze of publicity and a welter of superfluous advice. David Wood of the *Times* advised her 'to learn to resist hats . . . It is common to see the most serious arguments of women members invalidated not by ministerial replies but by flippant accessories. Aim from the beginning at a vivid simplicity, Mrs Ewing, for whatever the constitution says, you will be a guest in an essentially male club'.[50] Her response was quick:

> I hope, and intend, to make my impact on the Commons by what I say and do, rather than by what I wear. Nevertheless, clothes are important . . . so I have chosen a matching coat and dress in bright purple for this ceremonial occasion. I shall go into Westminster with my head held high – not for myself but for the thousands of people who have taken heart from this victory.[51]

Despite individual acts of kindness from Gwynfor Evans, Gwynneth Dunwoody, Sir Alex Douglas Home and some Liberal MPs she found being the only Scottish Nationalist at Westminster between 1967 and 1970 'a hideous experience':

> Westminster is very cruel. Being in a minority of one gives an acid test of the system. You have to be very courageous or they'll break you. I was important because I had won a safe Labour seat. Donald Stewart didn't represent the same kind of threat when he was at Westminster alone. He was male anyway and a lot of the bullying I got was because I was a woman who had won a safe Labour seat . . .
> . . . I hated the House of Commons . . . If I made a speech there were

catcalls and abuse; at question-time there was similar rudeness. The English MPs didn't participate. Oliver Brown, a nationalist wit, said on my election that 'a shiver ran along the Scottish Labour benches looking for a spine to run up' . . . 'I thought the honourable lady had emigrated' was Willie Ross's first response to any question from me . . .
. . . I had expected to link up with Gwynfor Evans, the Plaid Cymru MP, and he was a great friend but he wasn't in the House of Commons much. He wasn't pursued by the Labour Party in the way that I was and he would say, 'The votes are in Wales, and I'll be there next week' . . . When Hamilton went back to Labour in 1970 I picked up the pieces of my life.[52]

Apart from the pressures of Westminster Winnie Ewing spoke at innumerable public meetings throughout Scotland. This reflected the rise of the SNP from the status of a minor party to that of a third party 'by 1970 at the latest'.[53] It all made for a steep learning curve for a woman who had spoken at few political meetings before being persuaded to stand as the Hamilton by-election candidate. She acknowledges, 'It was fearsome. I had no researcher, no helper, and hundreds of people hanging on my every word'.[54] Although she was a promising court lawyer much was made of the fact that she was a young married woman of 38 with three young children, Terence then aged four, Annabelle, seven, and Fergus, ten.[55] Her influence as a role model for other nationalist women has been immense, not simply because she won the Hamilton by-election but because it marked the beginning of a lengthy political career. She served as MP for Moray and Nairn from February 1974 until 1979, and as the Highlands and Islands Euro-MP from 1979 while holding numerous party posts, currently that of party President. Known in Europe as 'Madame Ecosse' her hold on the Highlands Euro-seat is widely reckoned to be based on a personal rather than a party vote. Keith Webb identified her as 'probably the first nationalist leader to attain individual prominence'.[56] She believes, 'My becoming an MP certainly influenced my party in giving encouragement to other women. I was able to become an MP as a mother of three young children'.[57]

'A TRADITION OF WOMEN?'

So how far has the SNP developed a 'tradition of women' since making an electoral breakthrough after 1967? A total of three Nationalist women MPs have been elected: Winnie Ewing; Margo MacDonald; and Margaret Bain (now Ewing). Winnie Ewing encouraged several other women to become parliamentary candidates. Margaret Ewing recently described being 'hijacked by my now mother-in-law at a National Council meeting in the early 1970s'.[58] Maureen Watt had a similar experience.[59] Winnie Ewing was re-elected in February 1974 as MP for Moray and Nairn. She snatched victory from the jaws of defeat in 1979 when, after losing her Westminster seat, she became Highlands and Islands MEP. Margo MacDonald was briefly MP for Govan. After her sensational by-election win in November 1973 she was dubbed the 'Blonde Bombshell' and much photographed with her two young daughters. Margaret Bain became MP for Dumbarton East in October 1974 by the narrowest of margins – 22 votes. This rapid procession of nationalist women MPs in the 1970s did a great deal to associate the SNP with women. One elector told Margaret Bain in 1974 'Between you, and Janette Jones and Phyllis Watt, if you all get elected, you'll nag the House of Commons into giving Scotland independence!'[60] The SNP put up more women candidates than all the other parties combined in 1970 and the highest number of women at the 1974 elections as Table 1 shows.

The three Nationalist women MPs undoubtedly encountered sexist attitudes. Winnie Ewing's 'daily crucifixions' at Westminster from 1967–70 partly illustrate this. First elected as relatively young women of 29, both Margaret Bain and Margo MacDonald had to fight against being stereotyped as 'dolly birds'. Both also separated from their then husbands during the 1970s. Barbed comment on her separation followed Margo MacDonald during her unsuccessful Hamilton by-election campaign in 1978. *Scotsman* columnist Julie Davidson wrote 'While opaque pundits were asking: "Will Hamilton deliver the coup de grace to the SNP?" you asked yourself if no-one would deliver the coup de grace to sexism and the double standard. Sexism can be male or female. "Where's Mr MacDonald, then?" shrieked a venomous woman, weeding her garden as Margo passed'.[61] Comment on Margo MacDonald sometimes appears particularly sexist – 'this hard-hitting, tough talking, oil-grabbing, splendidly constructed woman who detests being summed up by the size of her bra (37)'.[62] She later commented, 'I was very conscious at that time (1973) that other politicians regarded me as "a clever wee lassie", rather than their equal. But I'd had to get over that hurdle with my colleagues in Scotland and I did it by knowing just as much if not more than they did about the goals we were striving for'.[63] Her success in establishing herself as a propagandist was clear at the Hamilton by-election. The posters simply called her 'Margo' and as the *Scotsman* asked, 'Are there other politicians in Scotland who can afford to excise their names from electioneering posters?'.[64]

Margo MacDonald herself was clear that she thought of 'women in politics as politicians' but reluctantly had 'to concede that the majority of people regard them as a rather different group of politicians'. Her view was that women 'should be able to tackle economic, industrial and planning problems with the same interest and confidence as . . . male colleagues. If she cannot, she will not be treated as an equal politician – she will be "a

Table 1
SCOTLAND: Women candidates and MPs; General Elections 1918–1992

Election	Comm	Con & Un	Green	Labour	Liberal	Lib Dem	National Liberal	Others	SDP	SNP	TOTAL	Elected
1918	–	–	–	–	–	–	–	1	–	–	1	Nil
1922	–	–	–	–	2	–	1	–	–	–	3	Nil
1923	–	2	–	–	1	–	–	–	–	–	3	1 Un
1924	–	3	–	2	1	–	–	–	–	–	6	1 Un
1929	2	3	–	4	–	–	–	–	–	–	9	1 Lab / 1 Un
1931	1	4	–	4	–	–	–	1	–	1	10	3 Un
1935	–	4	–	2	2	–	–	1	–	–	9	2 Un
1945	–	3	–	3	1	–	–	1	–	–	8	3 Lab
1950	1	4	–	4	5	–	–	1	–	–	15	3 Lab / 1 Un
1951	–	3	–	6	–	–	–	–	–	–	9	3 Lab / 1 Un
1955	–	4	–	8	–	–	–	–	–	–	12	3 Lab / 1 Un
1959	–	3	–	5	1	–	–	–	–	–	9	3 Lab / 2 Un
1964	2	2	–	5	–	–	–	1	–	–	10	3 Lab / 2 Un
1966	4	3	–	3	1	–	–	–	–	–	11	1 Con / 3 Lab

Table 1 continued

1970	1	2	–	3	3	–	–	–	10	19	1 Con 1 Lab
Feb 1974	1	5	–	5	2	–	–	–	8	21	1 Con 1 Lab 1 SNP
Oct 1974	1	5	–	7	2	–	–	–	8	23	1 Con 1 Lab 2 SNP
1979	2	4	–	4	7	–	–	–	6	26	1 Lab
1983	1	7	2	3	5	–	–	5	9	32	1 Con 1 Lab
1987	–	12	3	3	7	–	–	9	6	40	1 All (Lib) 1 Lab 1 SNP
1992	–	11	6	6	–	22	5	–	15	65	3 Lab 1 Lib Dem 1 SNP

Source: these figures have been compiled with reference to F. W. S. Craig, *Scottish Parliamentary Election Manual* (Edinburgh, 1966); F. W. S. Craig, *Minor Parties at British Parliamentary Elections, 1885–1974* (London, 1975); and the *Times Guides to the House of Commons, 1970, 1974, 1979, 1983, 1987, and 1992* (London, 1970, 1974, 1979, 1983, 1987, and 1992).

woman in politics"'. Yet she implicitly acknowledged that women were not on an equal footing with men, finding it 'so UNFAIR that, even in 1975, the standards applied to women should be so much more exacting . . . Now what they [men] look like is of no importance . . . their FEMALE equivalents in appearance – no matter how politically astute or how socially caring – have the proverbial snowball's chance of being chosen by a selection committee of their party, whichever one it is. Women politicians with warts need not apply!' Women also had to be particularly good speakers 'since their sex is already something of a distraction from what they're trying to say or do'. She went on to comment wryly on the weight of domestic responsibilities:

> It's taken for granted that if a man has something special to offer in politics, his wife will create a home-life as a base for him. The same is not true for a woman.
> But if a woman politician was rash enough to admit that her absorption in politics made it impossible to have any interest in home-making, she would NEVER get elected – anywhere . . .
> . . . Unless a husband appreciates his wife as a politician as well as a woman, he probably won't be willing to shoulder more of the household responsibility than men traditionally do, particularly in Scotland.[65]

Margo MacDonald described herself as an 'ordinary' Scottish woman MP used to coping with her own household and like other working women she clearly faced 'double burdens'. This experience, however, is not unique to SNP women MPs. It has been commented that with the exception of Winnie Ewing 'most of the other active SNP women are professional women who don't have families'.[66] Margaret Ewing recently said 'It is good for the image of the SNP that it has had women representatives . . . I think that it has been encouraging for other women in the party to be able to "look at Winnie, Margaret and Margo" . . .'[67] But does this really amount to a tradition of women?

Since the formation of the NPS/SNP 40 individual women have contested parliamentary seats for the party. Its record since 1970 of putting up women candidates compares well with the more established Conservative and Labour parties although these parties have returned more women MPs. The numbers involved are low for all of the parties and some regard them as statistically insignificant. There has been a total of only 14 Nationalist MPs. Thus the three female MPs represent by far the highest proportion of women returned among all the parties. Yet this high proportion simply reflects the low totals of Nationalist MPs returned. The typical SNP counter to this is that 'If the SNP gets more MPs, then we will get more SNP women MPs. The SNP has a good record of putting up women candidates . . . two of the four seats which the SNP statistically stood a good chance of winning at the last election [1992] – the Western Isles, Perth & Kinross, Galloway & Upper Nithsdale, and North Tayside – were fought by women candidates'.[68] The 1992 election also introduced a new generation of Nationalist women candidates; 13 of the 15 SNP women candidates were fighting their first parliamentary campaign. Despite the striking by-election successes of Winnie Ewing and Margo MacDonald, however, in all, only seven women have fought by-elections for the SNP: Elma Campbell (1931); Mary Dott (1947); Winnie Ewing (1967); Margo MacDonald (1973 and 1978); Isobel Lindsay (1978); Kay Ullrich (1994); and Roseanna Cunningham. Further research will uncover the position in local government. It is likely to involve more women since local government has a higher level of female participation than Westminster. Since 1974 the proportion of women councillors in Scottish District Councils has risen from 12.9% in 1974 to 19.6% in 1988, and 22% in 1992, clearly an improvement on the Westminster figures.[69]

The SNP opposes quotas to ensure the selection of female candidates, strongly opposing the measure of having all-woman shortlists in 50% of non-Labour seats recently adopted by the Labour party in Scotland. It supports the introduction of a system of proportional representation with a top-up list. There is considerable wariness inside the SNP not only over issues such as quotas but over the wider question of women's issues. Individual women may be strongly supportive of, say, abortion rights, but the matter is one of individual conscience not of party policy. Flora McLean explained 'The SNP focus is more on women's rights as part of human rights'.[70] This approach is of long standing. Janette Jones, SNP candidate for Stirling West at the 1974 and 1979 elections, declared 'I'm not a feminist. I'm a personist'.[71]

Unsurprisingly there have been 'past and present fears that the Women's Forum might become a feminist clique . . . There was certainly a lot of resistance in the early 80s to setting up a Women's Forum. It was won then on the basis that since it would provide useful experience and training, why shouldn't we have it? And also on the basis that the party is big enough now to cater for women who want to have that kind of involvement'.[72] Its role is limited as Allison Hunter, SNP Director of Organisation, explained: ' . . . [it] meets on an annual basis. Although it reports back to the party at large it has no delegates to annual conference unlike the trade union group which has delegates to National Council, the National Executive, and national conference. The Women's Forum is not a power base but an interest group'.[73]

The basis of future approaches to women can perhaps be detected in

the work of the recently founded equal opportunity group. It has moni-
tored the gender division of party office-bearers, ensured the provision of
creches, and of taking women along to meetings, and checking that times
and venues of meetings suit women as far as possible. It also wishes to
promote the idea of job-sharing and job-shadowing in the constituencies.
Its Convenor, Maureen Watt, believes 'It is important to have women seen
as spokespersons. I think that the party is likely to increase its support
among youth because it's seen as a youthful party. I think that we have to
do the same for women'.[74] The SNP has also recently paid some attention
to the idea that women may be the missing ingredient in a nationalist
breakthrough from 'third' to 'major' party status.[75] Targeting women voters
has been vital for the main parties since 1918. Nationalist leaflets of the
1920s show that they too were aware of the need to appeal to women
although the party seems to have made few specific appeals to women since
then. A report to the party's National council in December 1992 noted that:

> There has been much comment since the general election [1992]
> about how the SNP has yet to attract women voters and that we need
> to improve our showing amongst women voters to improve our total
> vote. Cynics might say 'It figures'.[76]

The report made to National Council in 1992 suggested that 'if the SNP
continues to present far more men than women as its elected representatives . . . we ourselves are adding to the presentation of politics as a man's
world'.[77] A gender audit of the party made in 1992 found that:

> The representation [of women] at ordinary party membership level
> is the best, 40%. The representation decreases the 'higher' up the
> party structure you go, eg, 26% women candidates at 1992 districts,
> 12% European elections 1989, 44% National Council members, 17%
> Senior office bearers.[78]

The report concluded that 'unless we get our own house in order,
we will be presenting to the women of Scotland a Parliament of men
in Edinburgh not much different in make up than the Parliament of
men in Westminster. Is that an attractive offer for the women we need
to vote for us to deliver Independence?'[79]

This poses an intriguing dilemma to the SNP in the sense that delivering
independence is what the SNP is all about. It will be most interesting to see
what appeals to women materialise – or whether the SNP will continue to
rely on having women representatives to appeal to women.

WOMEN AND THE NATIONAL IDENTITY MIRROR

In this context it may be helpful to briefly examine the position of women in other nationalist movements and the relation of women to the debate on the Scottish national identity. Nationalist movements elsewhere have had varied impacts on women's lives as a comparison of earlier nationalist movements with emergent nationalism in Eastern Europe shows. In the context of examining the Indian national movement Kumari Jayawardena remarks on 'the essential conservatism of what on the surface seemed like radical change . . . the movement gave the illusion of radical change while women were kept in the structural confines of family and society . . . Women in the nationalist struggle did not use the occasion to raise issues that affected them as women'.[80] A contrast is offered by the example of Turkey where Kemal's reforms were cited 'all over the world as successful attempts at achieving women's emancipation from above . . . the reforms were an integral part of an attempt to force Turkey into the 20th century through the modernisation of all its institutions'.[81] After the enfranchisement of women in local elections in 1930 and in national elections in 1935, 18 women were elected (4.5%) to the Assembly. This was the highest number of women deputies in Europe at that time, when women did not have the vote in many countries including France and Italy.[82]

The recent setting up of new parliaments in Eastern Europe, in which emergent nationalism has played an important role, however, saw women's representation fall dramatically. Despite the introduction of PR electoral systems women's representation tumbled in the new democracies – from 32.2% to 20.5% in the then GDR, from 21% to 8.5% in Bulgaria, from 20.9% to 7% in Hungary, from 29.5% to 6% in Czechoslovakia, and from 34.3% to 3.5% in Romania.[83] Yet commenting upon the impact of perestroika upon the former Soviet republics Mary Buckley found that 'More than ever before in Soviet history, the nature of women's political activity and its future depends upon the women themselves'.[84] Women in Sajudis, the Lithuanian nationalist group, have developed a distinctive view of desirable political change, 'Men in Lithuania should conduct political struggle, while women should create a beautiful home. There is no point in having an autonomous Lithuania if home life is not improved'.[85] This is partly linked with a strong desire to reject perceived Russian control over areas of their lives, hence, for instance, opposition to creches. Buckley goes on to point out that 'not all nationalist movements, however, have conservative women's groups. Female activists who live in Kiev began in 1990 to meet to hold special women-only meetings . . . to discuss feminist and ecological issues . . . they experienced disapproval from some male nationalists'.[86] The implications of this variety of experiences of nationalist women for women in Scotland might also draw on the conclusion which Hanham arrived at in 1969:

It follows ... that the independent Scotland envisaged by the SNP would be very like the present Scotland, except it would be better governed and have a focus of national loyalty. In this sense the SNP must be regarded as a much more conservative body than its critics on the left and the right are inclined to make out. The nearest parallel is to be found in the old colonial empire, where dominion status or independence simply meant the transfer of power to a new group of politicians, while the structure of the state and of society was but little changed.[87]

In the Third World nationalism has been clearly linked to trying to shake off imperial domination. A common experience of all the countries discussed in Kumari Jayawardena's broad study of women and nationalism is that 'All had faced the reality of foreign conquest, occupation or aggression'.[88] This comment applies to the new states emerging from the collapse of the former Soviet Union. The Scottish situation was arguably similar during the wars with England between 1296 and 1400 – years recognised as formative of a very modern form of Scottish national identity – although the present situation is different. The intervening years have given the Scottish national identity debate its particular cast. Edwin Muir wrote in the 1930s that '. . . there seems to be no palpable hindrance to the union of Scotland as a nation. If there was a really strong demand for such a union, England could not withhold it, nor probably attempt to do so. The real obstacle to the making of a nation out of Scotland lies now in the character of the people, which is a result of their history . . . And that obstacle, being the product of several centuries of life, is a serious one; it is, in fact, Scotland'.[89] In 1970 Tom Nairn confronted the 'obstacle' writing bitterly that '"Scotland will be reborn the day the last Minister is strangled with the last copy of the Sunday Post. I hope I'm not alone" . . . this cry of rage has turned into a national joke . . . Joke Nation? Any outsider will see the paradox at once. The most significant thing is who is not being strangled: an Englishman . . . This betrays something crucial about Scottish identity. Scotland is not a colonised culture, but a self-colonised one . . . Unlike nearly all other colonised or forcibly assimilated peoples, the Scots really do have mainly themselves to blame, and so mainly themselves – or a part of themselves – to attack and destroy'.[90] Thus according to Nairn self-colonisation has produced 'that frightful sense of paralysis and doom where so many of our identity-games (and our political conversations) end up'.

The terms of the discussion of the Scottish national identity this century have been mainly manly to say the least. Nairn goes on to refer to 'the sense of castration'[91] and to round up the usual twentieth-century literary suspects in the identity game, MacDiarmid and McIlvanney, stressing 'That Drunk Man Looking at the Thistle in the 1920s was almost any Scottish literary intellectual looking in the identity-mirror from then to the present'.[92] Women have not necessarily rejected this. In 1933 Marian McNeill went so far as to bless it!

> 'What Scotland needs', I heard a patriotic Scot exclaim a few years ago, 'is brutal young men'. Luckily the brutal young men have emerged. Of course, they are not popular – they would be of no use to us if they were – but I venture to prophesy that a generation will arise and call them blessed. They include such men as C. M. Grieve, George Malcolm Thomson, Donald Carswell, and Dewar Gibb.[93]

The contributions of women writers such as Willa Muir, Naomi Mitchison and Catherine Carswell have been neglected. In a recent article, 'No Gods and Precious Few Women', Alexandra Howson argued that 'within debates concerning Scottish identity, either those which assert that Scotland is framed as inferiorist or those which allude to the positive images which may be provided by a reclamation of working class history, women are marginalised and femininity is selectively deployed as a symbolic category'.[94] The lack of prominence given to Scotswomen or of prominent Scotswomen has been commented upon in a range of ways. MacDiarmid asserted that 'Scottish women of any historical interest are curiously rare . . . our leading Scotswomen have been . . . almost entirely destitute of exceptional endowments of any sort'.[95] In 1979 Julie Davidson commented that the Scotswoman had become epitomised as 'Ma Broon . . . She haunts the sculleries and parlours of Scotland's social history like an irreversible curse. She patrols our psyche like a bossy traffic warden, comic incarnation of the authoritarian drudge. She is Margaret Ogilvie writ large, speaking in balloons, the martyred mother figure who stalks the pages of Scottish literature. She is Black Agnes of the but-and-ben, scolding her menfolk, stiffening their backbones, sacrificing herself and her daughters on the altar of their incompetence. She's even bigger than the men'.[96] In much this vein she wrote about Margo MacDonald after the Hamilton by-election defeat in 1978:

> Margo is her mother's daughter re-shaped. She is the articulate, political expression of a familiar figure on the Scottish landscape – the tough household administrator who, by necessity, is part-drudge and part-bully. While the Margo's mothers of the country put their homes in order, the Margos perceive the chore as a national one.[97]

In 1980 Margaret Bain argued that such marginalisation of women was linked to national 'self-belittlement . . . these sophisticated nuances which have denigrated Scottishness account for much of the lack of prominence given to Scots women. For in a society which is essentially repressive and lacking in confidence, the weaker sections will be even more repressed and their achievements even more ignored . . . Yet, how essentially undeserved is this description of self-belittlement. Because in the perpetuation of the image of noble sacrifice we are, as women, demeaning our achievements and stultifying the potential for progress. The longer we adhere to that image, the longer it will take for Scotswomen to assert themselves in greater numbers in public life. It reeks of the same brutalising under-estimation of self and nation which creates the drunken hooliganism in the wake of Wembley, Hampden, Twickenham and Murrayfield internationals'.[98]

The mixed lesson on change for women from other nationalist movements and attitudes to women within the debate on Scottish national identity represents a challenge for nationalist women who presumably have a special interest in reshaping the Scottish national identity via independence. So far this challenge has been recognised particularly in the literary context. In 1980 the Scottish literary magazine *Chapman* published *Woven by Women*, recently described as 'something of a milestone, a landmark, a watershed, as the first Scottish publication to focus on women's cultural achievement across the artistic spectrum in Scotland'.[99] Subsequent editions of *Chapman* have paid welcome attention to the work of Scottish women writers reflecting wider efforts to rescue 'the tales of our grandmothers'.[100] Canongate publishers have performed an invaluable service to Scottish literature in reprinting many excellent Scottish novels including those of women writers. Yet in the political context, given past and present attitudes, it seems unlikely that the SNP will attempt to raise women's issues as such. SNP women have put nationalism itself at the top of their agenda.

CONCLUSION

Inevitably the conclusions arrived at here are tentative as this paper is written at an early stage of ongoing research. The main aim of this article has been to begin to address the historical neglect of women's involvement in Scottish nationalism. Future study will have a bearing on questions relating to women's participation in the political process and on the distinctive part played in that process by nationality.

Women have played an active role within the NPS and the SNP since 1934, mostly as 'part-time voluntary workers in constituency associations'. The role of by-elections in the rise of the SNP from the 1960s has drawn in constituency activists from all over the country. Women such as Isa Fisher turned out regularly to campaign for the party in every election. A founding member of the SNP she died early in 1994 leaving the SNP a small fortune in her will. Allison Hunter recalled with affection 'She worked in Govan in 1988 and at the Glasgow Central by-election where she ran a tea-room. To the younger activists she was known as "Attilla the Tea Lady" because you were only allowed half an hour, then she was up and at you to get back to work!'[101] Margo MacDonald suggested that at the constituency level 'there is a distinctive feminine point of view'[102] and an aim of future research will be to explore this. Future research will also focus on the part played by women in local government and on SNP structures including candidate selection procedures. More detailed attention will be paid to the influence women have had on the development of party policy and within the SNP leadership (for instance, Margaret Ewing's unsuccessful leadership bid in 1990). Present SNP women activists appear particularly optimistic about their ability to take on their chosen roles within the SNP although some limitations are acknowledged. For instance, six out of ten places on the party's National Executive are currently held by women but as Kathleen Caskie pointed out 'There is a ceiling between the National Executive and the Vice-Convenors. The Vice-Convenors are all men. Most of the men are in their 40s as it takes some time to get to these positions'.[103]

The party has undoubtedly benefited, perhaps unduly, from the high profile of its three past and present women MPs and the Hamilton by-election in 1967 appears as a crucial turning point in the SNP's record on putting up women parliamentary candidates. Only two women, Elma Campbell and Mary Dott, contested seats for the nationalists between 1928 and 1967. The numbers of women candidates improved significantly after the Hamilton by-election. As Margaret Ewing comments, 'I think that tradition [of SNP women candidates] goes back to Winnie. I don't know if things would have been different if a man had won Hamilton for the SNP'.[104] The question is hypothetical but the answer is surely 'Yes'. The follow-up question is 'What next?' If the SNP is to retain its association with women it has to move beyond Winnie, Margo and Margaret. The outcome of the forthcoming Perth and Kinross by-election and of the next general election will give some indication not only of the prospects of nationalism but of women within the nationalist movement.

University of St Andrews.

[I would like gratefully to acknowledge the support given to me by the Glenfiddich Fellowship; and the research travel grant awarded to me by the British Academy].

1   *Glasgow Herald*, 3 April 1978.

2   For a comparative overview of women's representation see J. Lovenduski & J. Hills (eds), *The Politics of the Second Electorate: Women and Public Participation – Britain, USA, Canada, Australia, France, Spain, West Germany, Italy, Sweden, Finland, Eastern Europe, USSR, Japan* (London, 1981).

3   This calculation is based on election statistics drawn from F. W. S. Craig, *British Electoral Facts, 1832–1987* (Aldershot, 1989), *passim*; and *The Year Book for Scotland 1966* (Edinburgh, 1966), *passim*.

4   For a discussion of the recent debates on Scottish women's representation within the Scottish Constitutional Convention in particular see C. Levy (now Burness), 'A Woman's Place?: A Future Scottish Parliament', in D. McCrone & L. Paterson (eds), *The Scottish Government Yearbook 1992* (Edinburgh, 1992).

5   M. Bain, 'Scottish Women in Politics', *Chapman*, 27–28, Summer 1980, p. 8. As Chancellor of the Exchequer in 1888 Goschen introduced a population percentage formula upon which government expenditure in Scotland was based, known since as the Goschen Formula.

6   F. W. S. Craig, *Minor Parties at British Parliamentary Elections, 1885–1918* (London, 1975), p. 89.

7   *The Scots Independent*, October 1927, p. 12.

8   *Ibid*, February 1929, p. 41.

9   *Ibid*.

10 *Home Rule for Scotland – The Case in 90 Points* (Glasgow, 1922), p. 97. Thanks to Dr Richard Finlay for this reference.

11 *The Scots Independent*, April 1929, p. 72.

12 See C. Burness, 'The Long Slow March; Scottish Women MPs, 1918–1945', in E. Gordon & E. Breitenbach (eds), *Out of Bounds* (Edinburgh, 1992), for a discussion of main party appeals to women voters in the interwar years.

13 R. J. Finlay, 'Pressure Group or Political Party? The Nationalist Impact on Scottish Politics, 1928–1945', *20 Century British History*, Vol 3, No 3, 1992, p. 276.

14 *The Scots Independent*, May 1929, p. 82.

15 *Ibid*, October 1928, pp. 174–5.

16 Interview with Lt Col (ret) Muriel Gibson; 12 October 1993.

17 *The Scots Independent*, January 1929, p. 26.

18 *Ibid*, January 1930, p. 28.

19 *Ibid*, July 1932, p. 140.

20 *Ibid*, August 1932, p. 159.

21 *Ibid*, December 1932, p. 22.

22 *Ibid*, August 1932, p. 152.

23 *Ibid*, January 1930, p. 28.

24 F. W. S. Craig, p. 89.

25 K. Webb, *The Growth of Nationalism in Scotland* (Glasgow, 1977), p. 61.

26 M. Fry, *Patronage and Principle* (AUP, 1991), p. 180.

27 J. MacCormick, *The Flag in the Wind* (London, 1955), p. 128.

28 H. J. Hanham, *Scottish Nationalism* (London, 1969), p. 179.

29 Interview with Lt Col (ret) Muriel Gibson.

30 Interview with Nancy Forsyth, 3 August 1993.

31 H. J. Hanham, p. 177.

32 *The Midlothian Advertiser*, 5 September 1952.

33 Interview with Maureen Watt, 24 September 1993.

34 W. Wood, *Yours Sincerely for Scotland* (London, 1970), p. 59.
35 W. Wood, p. 198.
36 *Ibid*, p. 63.
37 *Ibid*, p. 198.
38 Interview with Anne Raitt, 12 October 1993.
39 *The Midlothian Advertiser*, 5 September 1952.
41 Interview with Nancy Forsyth.
42 K. Webb, p. 99.
43 H. J. Hanham, p. 204; and K. Webb, p. 100.
44 H. J. Hanham, p. 184.
45 *Ibid*, p. 182.
46 Interview with Winnie Ewing, 4 August 1993.
47 H. J. Hanham, p. 185.
48 Interview with Ruth Marr, 25 September 1993.
49 Interview with Margaret Ewing, 30 June 1993.
50 *Times*, 6 November 1967.
51 *Daily Record*, 14 November 1967.
52 Interview with Winnie Ewing.
53 R. Levy, *Scottish Nationalism at the Crossroads* (Edinburgh, 1990) discusses 'minor' and 'third' party status and the rise of the SNP to 'third' party status in the 1970s, pp. 3–6.
54 *Ibid*.
55 *Daily Telegraph*, 6 November 1967.
56 K. Webb, p. 101.
57 Interview with Winnie Ewing.
58 *Snapshot*, Edition 7, p. 8.
59 Interview with Maureen Watt.
60 Interview with Margaret Ewing.
61 *Scotsman*, 5 June 1978.
62 *Daily Express*, 14 January 1976.
63 *Glasgow Herald*, 3 April 1978.
64 *Scotsman*, 5 June 1978.
65 *Scottish Daily News*, 14 May 1975.
66 Interview with Flora McLean, 2 July 1993.
67 Interview with Margaret Ewing.
68 Interview with Lari Don, 12 October 1993.
69 Information provided by the Scottish Local Government Information Unit based on statistics compiled by John Bochel & David Denver following the 1988 and 1992 District Council elections.
70 Interview with Flora McLean.
71 Interview with Ruth Marr.
72 Interview with Janet Law, 25 September 1993.
73 Interview with Allison Hunter, 12 October 1993.
74 Interview with Maureen Watt.
75 R. Levy discusses 'minor' and 'third' party status and the rise of the SNP to 'third' party status in the 1970s, pp. 3–6.
76 Report from Ms Maureen Watt, Convenor Equal Opportunities Sub-Committee, to Meeting of National Council on 5 December 1992, passim.
77 Report, Appendix IV, Comment on the SNP and Women.
78 *Ibid*.

79   *Ibid.*
80   K. Jawayardena, *Feminism and Nationalism in the Third World* (London, 1989ed), pp. 107–8.
81   *Ibid*, p. 41.
82   *Ibid*, p. 38.
83   *Guardian*, 25 July 1990.
84   M. Buckley, 'Gender and reform', in C. Merridale & C. Ward (eds), *The Historical Perspective: Perestroika* (London, 1991), p. 80.
85   *Ibid*, p. 70.
86   *Ibid*, p. 72.
87   H. J. Hanham, p. 212.
88   K. Jayawardena, p. 3.
89   E. Muir, *Scottish Journey* (London, 1985 ed, 1st pub 1935), pp. 233–5.
90   T. Nairn, 'Scottish Identity: A Cause Unwon', in *Chapman*, 67, Winter 1991/92, pp. 3–4.
91   *Ibid*, p. 8.
92   *Ibid*, p. 5.
93   *The Scots Independent*, April 1933, p. 84.
94   A. Howson, 'No Gods and precious few women: gender and cultural identity in Scotland', in *Scottish Affairs*, No. 2, Winter 1993, p. 48.
95   M. Bain, 'Scottish Women in Politics', in *Chapman*, 27–28, Summer 1980, p. 9.
96   *Scotsman*, 19 February 1979.
97   *Ibid*, 5 June 1978.
98   M. Bain, p. 4.
99   J. Hendry, Editorial, in *Chapman* 74–75, Autumn/Winter 1993, 'The Women's Forum: Women in Scottish Literature', p. 3.
100   A. Riddell, 'What happened to the tales of our grandmothers?', in Chapman 74–75, pp. 5–10.
101   *Scotsman*, 14 January 1994. Thanks to Mr Kevin Pringle, SNP Research Officer, for this reference.
102   *Scottish Daily News*, 14 May 1975.
103   Interview with Kathleen Caskie, 25 September 1993.
104   Interview with Margaret Ewing.

CATHERINE KERRIGAN

Desperately Seeking Sophia: Hugh MacDiarmid and the Female Principle

As the writer who has exercised the greatest single influence on modern Scottish literature, MacDiarmid presents problems to women critics committed to inscribing women's voices into a male-constructed canon. MacDiarmid, no less than his predecessors (and most of his successors), rarely treats female presence as anything other than the object of male desire. But what distinguishes MacDiarmid is his experience of woman as 'other', his sometimes profound sense of woman's power to disturb his secure world of masculine authoring.

In MacDiarmid's early poems, woman is invariably idealized as the object of MacDiarmid's meditations. Abstract female figures – Madonna, Muse and Goddess – predominate. These are all forms of the 'eternal feminine', that 'perfect' but static image of woman which Simon de Beauvoir in *The Second Sex* recognised as something to be equated with class and race labels, like 'the black soul' or 'the Jewish character'. Her objection to such labels is that they are dehumanising because they suggest a timeless, 'natural' order – a fixed immutable state – which disguises the social construction of female identities, as well as the power structures which maintain them.

The 'eternal feminine' is also the image of woman which informs symbols of nationhood. Collective values and traditions are enshrined in a female figure who represents all the virtues of ideal womanhood. In her role as symbolic mother she is both begetter and protector of the nation. Her 'natural' origins signify a long ancestry which is also connoted by her name which, as in Caledonia, is usually the nation's archaic name. She is revered for her strength and power while, paradoxically, women themselves are politically powerless.

In MacDiarmid's 'Within that Week' (a sonnet on the Creation myth), the eternal feminine is a 'slim white form' which a 'lonely' God calls into being. In the 'The Litany of the Blessed Virgin', it is the Madonna as the 'mystic rose' who invokes 'ecstasies no earthly tongue can tell'. These images are objects to be contemplated and worshipped because they offer MacDiarmid a route to the transcendental. 'Ecstasy' and 'mystery' are presented as the prime motives here, but all too often MacDiarmid's language betrays his desire for more down-to-earth pleasures, as in *from* 'Water of Life':

> Exult, one with the Bridegroom, in the plight
> Of the virginal year, O Soul,
> Opening her robe in the nuptial night,
> Gaining the lubric goal.
> Feast your eyes on the light
> Of hair of gold
> And body white
> – Yea, till you hold
> Earth, as a bridegroom holds his swooning, bare,
> Impregnate bride.
> Pleat you wild shivers on the quivering air,
> Insatiate tide,
> While in your seminal shower
> Dead wombs reflower.
>
> (*Complete Poems*, II, 1213–5)

The biblical union of bride and bridegroom is expressed here in erotic metaphors, and the experience is meant to be one of religious ecstasy. But it is hard to read lines like 'gaining the lubric goal' and 'Insatiate tide' without laughing. This 'ecstasy' has more than its fair share of pubescent enthusiasm. References to vibrating 'golden groins' (*from* 'Water of Life'), breasts which dangle on 'pale skies' ('Playmates') or 'whirling' breasts ('Spanish Girl') owe more to a testosterone rush than to poetic vision. When Macdiarmid wrote them he had not yet learned to laugh at himself 'within his courage bag confined'.

As his poetry developed, MacDiarmid, to some degree, began moving away from idealized female images, and his interest in Sophia, the symbol of wisdom in the gnostic and hermetic traditions (which he found in the work of the Russian philosopher, Vladimir Soloviev), suggests an attempt to introduce an active female principle into his poetry. To MacDiarmid, Sophia was 'not a mere lifeless image in God's mind, but a conscious and living entity – the Wisdom of God' (*Selected Essays*, p. 49).

In Proverbs 8: 24–36, Sophia is the female counterpart of the Creator, 'set up from everlasting, from the beginning'. She is the principle of incarnation which brings the material world into being, and as such she is often associated with nature goddesses like Persephone and Isis. Sophia also finds an equivalent in the Shekinah of the Kabbala tradition where, as M. H. Abrams argues, the female principle both modifies the 'austere male monotheism of Hebrew theology' and signifies 'sexuality in the very nature of God . . . the sacred union becomes a central and pervasive symbol which accounts for the origin and sustainment of life' (*Natural Supernaturalism*, p. 155). As Abrams suggests, the introduction of the female principle acknowledges sexual and reproductive activity through the union of contrasting principles, nevertheless the female principle is presented here only in her relation to the male behaviour she 'modifies': she is object, not subject.

Central to MacDiarmid's understanding of Sophia was the idea of 'syzygy' – change enacted through contrasting forces – and this (together with the ideas of Nietzsche and Spengler) helped him to articulate a theory of poetry and culture ('the Caledonian Antisyzygy') as essentially oppositional, and which he expressed in his famous battle-cry in *A Drunk Man Looks at the Thistle*, 'I'll ha'e nae hauf-way hoose, but aye be whaur/Extremes meet'. These extremes have been categorized in a number of ways by critics: the opposition of Scotland and England, Scots dialect and standard English, proletariat and bourgeoisie, and so on, but they have never been examined in terms of the oppositional male and female principles which are at the heart of his theory.

Of course, part of the problem is that MacDiarmid never related his interest in the female principle to contemporary events. Yet in the immediate pre- and post-war period it would have been impossible for MacDiarmid to be unaware of 'the woman question'. The Women's Social and Political Union, established by the Pankhursts in 1903, had active branches in Glasgow and Edinburgh, and the feminist campaign for 'Votes for Women' was being supported, as Elspeth King has documented, in the socialist journal *Forward*, of which MacDiarmid was an avid reader and supporter ('The Scottish Women's Suffrage Movement', p. 134). In a letter to his old schoolmaster, George Ogilvie, MacDiarmid does mention a particularly colourful Scottish feminist, Flora Drummond (1879–1949), who was known as 'The General' because she led suffragette parades riding on a horse (*The MacDiarmid/Ogilvie Letters*, p. 9). But MacDiarmid's own radical and reforming zeal did not extend to public support of the women's movement. He would certainly have known of Willa Muir's important feminist analysis, *Women: an Inquiry* (1925), but he never once refers to it.

Nancy Gish has argued that, in at least one instance, MacDiarmid was less than sympathetic to contemporary women artists who were writing about women's issues. MacDiarmid's first Scots poem, 'The Watergaw', appeared together with his review of Rebecca West's *The Judge* in the *Scottish Chapbook* (1922). The review is written in Scots and sets out to demonstrate the expressive superiority of Scots over English. MacDiarmid makes it very clear that the revitalization of Scots, which is now part of his agenda, is no job for a woman: this is strictly man's work. As Gish points out, this is a classic ploy of male control of language, for not only does the heroine, Ellen Melville, speak in 'distinctively Scottish rhythms and phrases' but also the book, much of which is based on West's personal experiences, is about 'illegitimacy, abandonment, marital rape, child abuse and women's oppression' ('Hugh MacDiarmid', *The Gender of Modernism*, p. 277). *The Judge* is also one of the few Scottish novels which deals with the women's movement of the 1920s in Edinburgh.

The desire to control West's language and ideas can be interpreted as MacDiarmid's own anxieties about women and their creativity, and is symptomatic of his own incapacity to deal with a feminist movement dedicated to displacing patriarchal power. That this movement was taking place at the time he was attempting to analyze and reconstruct Scottish national identity is significant.

A Drunk Man is MacDiarmid's attempt to write a national epic at a period (post World War One) when the very validity of the nation state was being called into question. The dispersed and fragmentary quality of the poem places it firmly in the modernist movement, and MacDiarmid, recognizing that destabilized identities were the very condition of post-war existence, played out the drama of his own fractured psyche in the persona of the Drunk Man.

The Drunk Man is the sole speaker of the poem, so it is only through his perceptions that we know of its two female figures, Jean and 'the silken leddy'. Jean is the man's wife who, like Kate o' Shanter, waits at home for her drunken husband. 'The silken leddy' or 'Goddess' is a version of Sophia and is introduced in the two lyrics adapted from Alexander Blok.

Jean is a fixed principle: she is a model of 'natural' goodness and solid domesticity, the stereotype of the always faithful, always dutiful wife. Although Jean does have the last words in the poem, we never hear her voice. What we know of Jean is strictly limited to the Drunk Man's projections of her as the perfect wee wifey.

The 'silken leddy' is completely voiceless but, unlike Jean, she is not a fixed figure; she is shape-changing, protean. The Drunk Man is drawn to her as to a siren; she is a mystery whose secret he wants to possess:

> I seek, in this captivity,
> To pierce the veils that darklin' fa'
> – See white clints slidin' to the sea,
> And hear the horns o' Elfland blaw.
>
> I ha'e dark secrets' turns and twists,
> A sun is gi'en to mee to haud,

The whisky in my bluid insists,
And speirs my benmaist history, lad.

And owre my brain the flitterin'
O' the dim feathers gangs aince mair,
And, faddomless, the dark blue glitterin'
O' two een in the ocean there . . .
(Complete Poems, I, p. 89)

The unattainable lady simultaneously attracts and repels. The Drunk Man both desires and fears her, and acknowledges that he is helpless to control her because she is part of his deepest anxieties.

The two women of *A Drunk Man* are opposites. In Jungian terms, Jean is the 'positive' side of the anima and embodies 'maternal solicitude and sympathy, the magic authority of the female, the wisdom and exaltation that transcend reason . . . all that is benign, all that cherishes and sustains, that fosters growth and fertility' (*Collected Works*, vol. IX, p. 82). The lady signifies 'anything secret, hidden, dark; the abyss, the world of the dead, anything that devours, seduces and poisons, that is terrifying and inescapable like fate' (*Collected Works*, vol. IX, p. 82).

In the two lyrics to the lady, it is the Drunk Man's darker side which is exposed in language. The lyrics are rhythmically very seductive but anxiety-ridden language keeps erupting: 'I ha'e dark secrets' turns and twists'; 'terror clings to me an unknown face'. The benign drunk of the opening becomes increasingly aggressive: 'dost thou mak' a thistle o' me, wumman?' The lady becomes his 'cursed Conscience'; *he* has transformed her into the 'Frankenstein that nae man can escape'. She is *his* self-created monster – the external image of his internal anxieties.

Yet there is an analogy between the lady's shape-changing, anxiety-inducing powers and the language of the poem. With its range of verses and vocabularies, its sudden transitions and intermissions, the poem lacks any 'traditional' structure: it does not follow the hierarchical pattern of male-dominated public discourse. According to Lacan and Kristeva's re-readings of Freud, language is ruled by a binary logic, that is, concepts like matter and form, head and heart, reason and emotion, phallus and vagina, objectivity and subjectivity are situated within the language in a hierarchical relationship: male principles are privileged and dominate language.

Lacan argues that this male domination of language posits woman as 'other'. At the same time, women's own writing is seen as unstructured, irrational and chaotic: it does not follow the linear, rational patterns of male discourse. The perception of women's language as chaotic is challenged by Kristeva who argues that this type of 'illogical' language points to a different order, and that this *l'ecriture feminine* is of a piece with the *avant garde* writing of moderns like James Joyce. MacDiarmid was certainly attracted to 'irrational' thinkers like Nietzsche, Shestov, Ouspensky, Gurdjieff – and Soloviev (the source of Sophia) – who critiqued and disrupted 'rational' modes of writing and philosophizing, and the influence of a number of them is found throughout *A Drunk Man*.

The chaotic language of *A Drunk Man* is localised in MacDiarmid's use of the symbol. Lacan argues that the symbolic order is essentially patriarchal: language develops at the time when the male child begins to separate from the mother, so in order to replace the lost mother, male language develops a symbolic order as a substitute, a way of referring to the absent 'other'. In this way, the symbolic is seen as a static order of patriarchal language. In *A Drunk Man*, the major symbols – thistle, moon, whisky, water, serpent – are not fixed; like 'the silken leddy', they constantly change shape – and meaning. Meaning is not presented in logical, 'rational', hierarchic terms; it is radically indeterminate and therefore subject to multiple interpretations. MacDiarmid's language is more semiotic than symbolic. In Lacan's theory of language development, the semiotic precedes the symbolic and is associated specifically with women because female children do not experience separation from the mother as the male does. The linguistic process of *A Drunk Man* is built on a series of floating signifiers which generate various constellations of potential meanings which are never contained in, or reduced to, one single 'truth'.

MacDiarmid's semiotics point to the psychic ambivalence of the poem: the Drunk Man's competing desire and loathing of the lady. What her appearances invariably signal is the beginning of the man's inner journey, a journey into a psychological dark continent. He enters into an imaginative space which, like the liminal landscapes of the ballads, is a place of magic and the supernatural, of shifting shapes and fractured identities. In this wilderness, there are no social and sexual codes, no signposts to mark the way forward or milestones to count progression. The boundary-crossing Drunk Man has entered the *terra incognita* of the female principle: he is confronted by his 'other'. In this new territory the 'leddy' becomes the Drunk Man's mirror image – his double.

In this landscape, the Drunk Man sees in that giant phallic symbol, the thistle, images of entrapment (the 'bindweed', the sea-monster). His sense of himself as man, poet, and nationalist becomes increasingly fragmented and he comes to understand that his only way forward is to confront and slay the monster within. But for all his bravado, this is precisely what the Drunk Man fails to do. He does not resolve the dilemma by himself, instead he looks to his wife Jean to rescue him.

At many points on the journey he has referred to Jean and their sexual partnership. In a *double entendre* he tells how she will know 'whence this thistle sprang', and of how he finds in her sexuality 'a kind o' Christianity'. Increasingly, Jean takes on the initial role of the goddess/lady as a source of higher spiritual experience and the Drunk Man now looks to his wife for 'the wisdom and exaltation that transcend reason'. Having moved from the divine to the domestic model, the Drunk Man believes Jean can unite his physical and spiritual desires, and she is thus enthroned as the ideal of her gender.

The 'silken leddy', on the other hand, takes on increasingly terrifying shapes as the man in his befuddled state tries to make sense out of what he is seeing. When he looks at the moon, 'To Luna at the Craidle-and-Coffin', she becomes the Carline who wants to 'stap me in your womb' (p. 109). She is an endless, devouring fecundity: 'Owre and owre, the same auld trick,/Cratur withoot climacteric!' (p. 109). The Drunk Man cannot come to knowledge about, or through, the lady: she can only continue to signify his deepest anxieties.

By the end of the poem, the lady has disappeared and the object of salvation, Jean, triumphs:

> Be thou the licht in which I stand
> Entire, in thistle-shape, as planned,
> And no hauf-hidden and hauf-seen as here
> In munelicht, whisky, and in fleshly fear
> (p. 146)

The Drunk Man returns to Jean as to a mother who will satisfy all his needs. Jean is reified as the national symbol: the ever-nurturing mother who will always comfort and protect. But the Drunk Man has evaded the very issues he raised – the cultural destitution and restructuring of the nation. True, in grand Romantic style, he has declared his intention of taking on 'the burden o' my people's doom', but at the end of the poem his retreat into 'Silence' signals a return to the transcendental – MacDiarmid's trusty escape-hatch. From the early poems to *A Drunk Man*, through *On a Raised Beach* and on to *In Memoriam James Joyce*, MacDiarmid always resolves his difficulties by moving to a higher spiritual sphere. In this rarefied atmosphere he can comfortably look down on and dismiss his many dilemmas. But the cost of doing that is the loss of any real change because in the end he fails to reconstruct either his own or his nation's identity. Similarly, although he articulates anxieties about the female 'other', the significance of this remains buried in his unconscious, and the image of woman at the end is predictable and stereotypical.

If the figuring of women in *A Drunk Man* is static and conservative, how can it be read as a progressive national narrative? The simple answer is it cannot, and certainly MacDiarmid recognised the poem's limitations in terms of his own nationalist ideals. *A Drunk Man* is less a rallying cry than a *cri de coeur*. Like other modernists (and nationalists) MacDiarmid could state the problem, but not the solution.

In attempting to define a new concept of nationalism, the MacDiarmid of *A Drunk Man* in the 1920s was occupying the same psychological space as women. As a writer of a marginalized and colonized country trying to liberate himself from a stronger, and globally more powerful, literary and political tradition, his position is identical to that of Scottish women who, internally colonized, have until recently played a very circumscribed part in Scotland's political, institutional and cultural life.

Yet it would be a mistake to dismiss *A Drunk Man* too quickly. In MacDiarmid's defence it has to be said that any categorical rejection of his work as ultra-chauvinist is undermined by poems which reveal a sensitive identification with women's experiences. As Pam Morris has recently pointed out, in 'Empty Vessel' MacDiarmid deals with a particular female experience (a young mother mourning the death of her child) with a sensitivity which defies identification of authorship by gender (*Literature and Feminism*, p. 85).

It is also impossible to ignore the extraordinary frequency with which babies keep appearing in MacDiarmid's poems – 'Empty Vessel', 'Bonnie Broukit Bairn', 'O Jesu Parvule', 'Lo, a Child is Born' – and his use of images and metaphors which relate to female physiology (particularly parturition), or by the way in which he did acknowledge that women poets like Marion Angus and Violet Jacob influenced his writing in Scots, or by the inclusion of so many women poets in his *Northern Numbers* anthologies.

Individually these acts may seem insignificant, but collectively they suggest that MacDiarmid was susceptible to the influence of women, and that at least part of his work represents an attempt at some level – conscious or unconscious – to explore the female side of his own personality.

University of Guelph

WORKS CITED

This paper has evolved from a presentation at a colloquium with the wonderfully oxymoronic title, 'Destabilising *A Drunk Man*', which was organised by graduate students at Edinburgh University in February, 1993. All references to MacDiarmid's poems are from the *Complete Poems*.

Abrams, M. H., *Natural Supernaturalism: Tradition and Revolution in Romantic Literature*, New York, Norton, 1971.

Beauvoir, Simone de, *The Second Sex*, tr. H. M. Parshley, Harmondsworth, Penguin, 1972.

Gish, Nancy, 'Hugh MacDiarmid, 1888–1978' in *The Gender of Modernism: A Critical Anthology*, Indiana University Press, 1990.

Jung, Carl, *Collected Works*, vol. IX, eds. Herbert Read, Michael Fordham, Paul Gerhard Adler, London, Routledge and Kegan Paul, 1951.

King, Elspeth, 'The Scottish Women's Suffrage Movement' in *Out of Bounds: Women in Scottish Society, 1800–1945*, eds. Esther Breitenbach and Eleanor Gordon, Edinburgh University Press, 1993.

MacDiarmid, Hugh, *Complete Poems, 1920–1976*, eds. W. R. Aitken and Michael Grieve, London, Martin Brian and O'Keeffe, 1978.

———, *The Hugh MacDiarmid/George Ogilvie Letters*, ed. C. Kerrigan, Aberdeen University Press, 1988.

———, *Selected Essays*, ed. Duncan Glen, London, Cape, 1969.

Morris, Pam, *Feminism and Literature*, Cambridge, Blackwell, 1993.

Notes on contributors

Douglas Dunn is the director of the St Andrews Scottish Studies Institute and Head of the School of English at the University of St Andrews. His last book of poems, *Dante's Drum-kit*, appeared in 1993 and he has just published a volume of short stories, *Boyfriends and Girlfriends*.

Marilyn Reizbaum teaches at Bowdoin College, Brunswick, Maine.

Anne M. McKim was educated at Dundee and Edinburgh Universities and is a Senior Lecturer in English at the University of Waikato, New Zealand. A founding member and currently treasurer of the Scottish Studies Association there, she teaches and publishes on early, mainly mediaeval, Scottish literature.

Aileen Christianson has worked on the Duke-Edinburgh edition of *The Collected Letter of Thomas and Jane Welsh Carlyle* since 1967, as an associate editor since volume 8 (1981), and is currently working on volume 25. She is also a lecturer in Scottish Literature at Edinburgh University.

Jan Pilditch is a lecturer in English at the University of Waikato, New Zealand. She has published on British and American writers and on writing by women. She is currently editing *The Critical Response to Katherine Mansfield*.

Eilidh Whiteford is a graduate of the universities of Glasgow and Guelph and is currently researching a doctoral thesis on Alasdair Gray at Glasgow University. The paper published in the present volume was prepared and written at the University of St Andrews in 1994.

Chris Gittings teaches Canadian and American literature and Canadian studies in the Department of American and Canadian Studies at the University of Birmingham. He has published articles on the cross-cultural dialogue between Canadian and Scottish literature. He is currently preparing a study of alterity in Canadian cinema.

S. J. **Boyd** is a lecturer in the School of English at the University of St Andrews. He has published articles on Alasdair Gray and Liz Lochhead.

Jean McNicol was born in Glasgow and brought up in Lenzie. She did an English degree at Oxford University and is now an assistant editor of the London Review of Books.

Catriona Burness (formerly Levy) is the Glenfiddich Research Fellow in the Department of Scottish History, University of St Andrews. She has written several articles on women in Scottish and British politics and is currently writing a history of women's involvement in Scottish party politics, 1880–1992.

Catherine Kerrigan teaches Scottish and English literature at the University of Guelph. Her publications include *Whaur Extremes Meet: the Poetry of Hugh MacDiarmid, 1920–1934*, *The Hugh MacDiarmid/George Ogilvie Letters*, *The Immigrant Experience* and *An Anthology of Scottish Women Poets*. She is general editor of the Centenary Edition of the Collected Works of Robert Louis Stevenson and has edited *Weir of Hermiston* and co-edited *The Ebb-Tide* with Peter Hinchcliffe.